Great Moments
in Pro Football

Detailed accounts of unusually dramatic or record-breaking performances in National Football League games. The topics range from the first NFL championship game to the first Super Bowl, and from the day Ernie Nevers scored forty points all by himself to the day Y.A. Tittle threw seven touchdown passes.

GREAT MOMENTS
IN PRO FOOTBALL

Compiled by
ZANDER HOLLANDER
Illustrated with photographs

RANDOM HOUSE
NEW YORK

Library of Congress Catalog Card Number: 77-90290
Manufactured in the United States of America

Photograph Credits:

John Biever: 136; Vernon J. Biever: front endpapers, viii, 18, 22, 42, 46,
49, 52, 92, 94, 98, 108, 112, 119, 163, 165, 167; Malcolm Emmons: vi,
32, 55, 58, 70, 72, 74, 160; Emmons & Brockway: 133; National Football
League Properties Photo Service: 145, 148, 149; New York Daily News
—Frank Hurley: 83; Ken Regan—Camera Five: 86, 155; Dan Rubin:
78; United Press International: 11, 24, 34, 64, 67, 102, 105, 110, 128,
142; Wide World: back endpapers, 7, 8, 30, 123, 134.

Cover photo (1969 Super Bowl): Vernon J. Biever

Contents

Introduction

Great moments in pro football can be the result of many things: an individual doing the impossible, a team achieving the improbable, or perhaps a game marking an historical occasion.

Gale Sayers runs with a football for the Chicago Bears. Jim Bakken kicks a football for the St. Louis Cardinals. Joe Namath throws a football for the New York Jets. Now Jim Brown plays leading roles in the movies. But he didn't make the lineup in this book because of his acting. Not long ago, Jim Brown was football's mightiest fullback, with the Cleveland Browns.

Like Namath, Sayers, Bakken and the others whose stories are told, Jim Brown is here because of something memorable that he did one day on the football field.

In the chapters that follow you will get to know the Iron Man (Chuck Bednarik) and the Bald Eagle (Y.A. Tittle), and you will have a seat at the Super Bowl and other historic games in such cities as Los Angeles, New York, New Orleans and Green Bay.

The Packers, with Bart Starr; the Jets, the Bears, the Cardinals, the Saints, the Giants, the Eagles, the Forty-Niners, the Chiefs, the Colts, the Rams, the Redskins, and the College All-Stars are some of the teams which have played a part in great moments of pro football.

Every fan vividly remembers a game or two that may be regarded as a "great moment." There are many more of them, of course, than can be covered in a single book. But some that aren't mentioned here may be found in other books in the Random House Punt, Pass and Kick Library.

A quarterback is important, but he needs supporting players. This quarterback thanks the following squad members for their contributions to *Great Moments in Pro Football*: Andy Carra, *Sport* Magazine; Murray Chass, Associated Press; Bill Guthrie, New Haven *Journal-Courier*; David Rosen, Associated Features; Bob Rubin, *Sport* Magazine; David Schulz, Associated Features, and Jack Zanger.

For their cooperation I also express my appreciation to Don Weiss and Buddy Young of the Pro Football Commissioner's office; Jim Heffernan, National Football League; Harold Rosenthal, American Football League; Dan Desmond of the Chicago Bears, and Ernie Nevers, one of the great athletes of all time.

Zander Hollander, Editor

Great Moments in Pro Football

1/Marshall's Folly

CHICAGO: December 17, 1933—Among the crowd of 26,000 fans who had come to Wrigley Field to see the first National Football League title game was George Preston Marshall, a laundryman from Washington, D. C. Marshall wasn't any ordinary laundryman, though. He was a laundry tycoon and he had used some of his money to purchase the NFL Boston Redskins. Once Marshall had the franchise he used his influence as an owner to revolutionize the game. The Redskins weren't playing in the NFL title game, however. The contest was between the Chicago Bears of the Western Division and the New York Giants from the Eastern Division. But without Marshall's influence in setting up such a playoff it is doubtful if *anybody* would have been present on the cold, windy Sunday in December.

Although he had been a team owner for only one year, Marshall had already inspired some of the most important rules changes in pro football history. He had convinced his fellow owners to move the goal posts back to the goal line where they had once been. This would enable place-kickers to try for a target 10 yards closer on their field-goal attempts. He also co-sponsored the new rule which allowed forward passing from anywhere behind the line of scrimmage instead of making the passer stand at least 5 yards behind the line.

Then, most important, he suggested a championship game.

Marshall had explained his proposed changes to the other owners at a meeting in Atlantic City. "I realize you men know your football inside and out," he said. "I know football only from a spectator's point of view. But that's exactly why I'm speaking to you. From a spectator's point of view, the kind of football you play makes a lousy show. It's dull, uninteresting and boring. The way I look at it, we're in show business. And when a show becomes boring to the public, you throw it out and put a more interesting one in its place. That's why I want to change the rules. I want to give the public the kind of show they want."

Marshall's radical theories would make the professional game different than the college version, and some of the owners protested that as long as the game was popular on the campuses there was no need to change it. Marshall insisted that his proposals would open up the game. Spectacular, long-gaining offenses would become possible and the field goal would be easier to achieve.

The owners finally agreed. And, as a result, Marshall was on hand at Chicago to see the more liberal forward passing in effect, to watch the field goal kickers aim at a closer target and, most important, to watch the first championship game in NFL history.

The Bears, who had finished with a 10-2-1 record in the West, were led by their awesome fullback Bronko Nagurski, a 238-pound battering ram from the University of Minnesota. His strength had already become an NFL legend, even though he was just completing his third pro season. Before the game someone asked Steve Owen, the Giant coach and right tackle, how he planned to stop Nagurski.

"With a shotgun as he comes out of the dressing room," Owen replied.

Nagurski wasn't the only Bear player Owen had to worry about. As a rule, any pro team that wins a championship is strong throughout the lineup, and Chicago was no exception. The Bears were savage hitters.

The Giants, were not without their big guns, either. The line anchored by Mel Hein was tough. Hein played center on offense and linebacker on defense. In the Giants' backfield, quarterback Harry Newman, an All-America from the University of Michigan, starred with halfback Ken Strong.

Together they provided a highly dangerous attack.

The two teams had already met twice during the regular season, a fact that only heightened the sense of excitement growing among the crowd of 26,000 fans assembled in Wrigley Field on the bleak December day. They had played each other to a standoff—the Bears winning the first meeting, 14-10, and the Giants taking the second, 3-0. The championship game would decide once and for all which was the better team.

The drama on the field began even before the opening kickoff. Quarterback Newman called the officials aside to check the legality of some trick plays his Giants were considering using. Assured they were legal, the visitors used one almost as soon as they got the ball—and almost got a touchdown.

The play was called the Hein Special because it involved a clever line shift that suddenly made the Giant center a temporary end. Newman took the snap from Hein on the Bear 45-yard line, handed it right back to him, then pivoted and "fell." The Bears were supposed to think the quarterback still had the ball and they did—until Hein, who was supposed to stroll down the field as casually as possible while his blocking formed, got excited at the sight of the open field in front of him. He began to run too soon, and was tackled on the Bear 15-yard line. There the Chicago defense stiffened and held the Giants from scoring. For a while, the trickery was abandoned—but only for a while. Before long

Bronko Nagurski made the Bears a powerful contender.

Harry Newman, the Giant quarterback, had some tricks up his sleeve for the championship game.

the Bears showed that they too could pull a rabbit or two out from under their helmets.

Late in the first quarter, the Chicago team returned a punt by Strong to the Giant 42-yard line. On the ensuing play, Nagurski faked a pass and bulled his way to the 26 for a 16-yard gain. A flock of Giants finally dragged Nagurski down. "The best way to stop him was to fall in front of him and trip him up," said Strong, who was in on the tackle.

"The only trouble was that you'd be wearing his cleat marks for weeks."

When the Bears were stopped on the Giant 16, Jack Manders came in to try a field goal. Manders, a rookie fresh from the University of Minnesota campus, had been given the nickname "Automatic Jack" because of the reliability of his kicking. On this particular day he deserved the compliment. His kick was perfect and the Bears led, 3-0. Midway through the second period Manders booted one from 40 yards out to make it 6-0, and the fans, who thought they sensed a rout in the making, began to scream for the Bears to turn it on.

A few minutes later the atmosphere in the bleachers changed. Suddenly Wrigley Field had all the gaiety and excitement of a funeral parlor. The Giants had refused to permit any rout. A 30-yard run by substitute halfback Kink Richards, followed by a 39-yard touchdown heave from Newman to Red Badgro, tied the score. Strong added the extra point and the visitors from New York left the field for the half-time intermission, leading 7-6. There were still thirty minutes to play, but already the tension was growing.

The lead changed hands three times in the third quarter, giving the spectators the feeling they were witnessing a ping-pong match. Early in the period, Nagurski raced 14 yards, then two plays later he roared 7 more yards to advance the ball to the Giant 39. George Corbett then passed to Carl

Brumbaugh, who ran to the 12. There the march was halted, and Automatic Jack came in to try a field goal from the 18. It was good, so the Bears led, 9-7.

Before anyone had time to celebrate, the Giants came storming right back on the strength of Newman's deadly passing. He hit Dale Burnett with a pass good for 23 yards. Then in the next play he hit him with a completion good for 13 yards to the Bears' 37. After an incompletion, the quarterback hit Richards on the 21 and completed one to Badgro on the 9. Then a penalty set the Giants back to the 14, but Newman came up with still another completion. This one was to Max Krause, who took it down to the 1-yard line. On the next day, Krause plunged over for a touchdown. The Giants were back in front, 14-9.

But the home team came storming back. Using Nagurski on straight power runs, the Bears marched straight down the field to the Giant 8-yard line. There they pulled their rabbit out from under their helmets, proving that they too could play the kind of spectacular, razzle-dazzle football that George Preston Marshall had envisioned.

Nagurski took a handoff and rushed up to the line as if the play was a plunge. But as the Giants massed to meet him, he stopped short, jumped high in the air and threw a dumpy little pass over everyone's heads to Bill Karr. Karr was standing alone in the end zone. The touchdown gave the Bears a 16-14

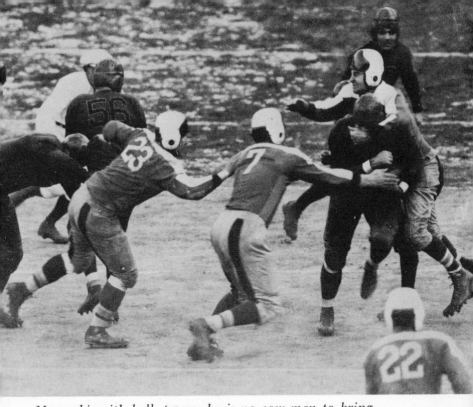

Nagurski, with ball, proves he is no easy man to bring down.

lead with just a few minutes to play in the third period. The fans roared their appreciation of their team's boldness.

But seconds later the roars turned to groans when the Giants bounced back. Newman completed four passes and advanced the ball to the Bears' 8-yard line as the third quarter came to an end.

On the first play of the final quarter, Strong put the Giants ahead again. It was the fifth time the lead had changed hands. In the process Strong showed why he was an all-time great. As he started an end sweep, he was hemmed in by the Bears, who appeared to be ready to throw him for a big loss. Realizing he was trapped, Strong improvised. He lateraled the ball to a surprised Newman heading the other way, then continued into the end zone. The alert Newman, spotting Strong all alone in the end zone, hit him with a touchdown pass. The Giants were ahead, 21-16, and time was running out.

Twice the Bears threatened and twice they were halted. Finally, a rare bad punt by Strong that carried only 9 yards gave Chicago the ball on the Giant 47-yard line. The crowd quieted to an eerie hush, sensing that this was probably Chicago's last chance.

The Bears moved to the Giant 33 in three plays. Then Nagurski got the ball again and started toward the line. The Giants suspected that this might be the time for the Bronk's jump pass, and they were right. But they couldn't anticipate the extra little twist the Bears had planned.

Nagurski tossed the ball to Bill Hewitt, one of the few players left in football who still refused to wear a helmet. Giant player Dale Burnett, diagnosing the play, rushed up and dumped Hewitt with a smashing tackle. Unfortunately Hewitt no longer had the ball. He had lateraled to Bill Karr, who was racing toward the goal line. Only Strong was near him.

The two men eyed each other carefully as they drew closer together. Carefully measuring the angle between himself, the goal and Karr, Ken Strong moved in closer and closer. A sure tackler, it seemed that Strong would nail his man—until Gene Ronzani carved a place for himself in football history by coming out of nowhere to dump Strong with a magnificent block. Karr raced untouched into the end zone to give Chicago a 23-21 victory and the NFL's first post-season championship.

For their efforts, the Bears received winning shares of $210.23 each—not much compared to the $15,000 a Super Bowl player gets now. But their game made football history.

2/Iron Man Bednarik

PHILADELPHIA: December 26, 1960—It was the day after Christmas. Chuck Bednarik's wife, Emma, and his four young daughters were still asleep when he climbed out of bed and tiptoed to the bathroom. It isn't easy for a man who stands 6-feet 3-inches tall and weighs 235 pounds to tiptoe from one room to another at 7 A.M. without disturbing his family. But Bednarik accomplished this with a minimum of effort as he showered and dressed.

He then crept quietly downstairs to the kitchen by way of the living room, where he had to avoid tripping over the children's new toys that were strewn on the floor near the Christmas tree. He plugged in the electric coffee percolator that Emma Bednarik had filled the night before and gently lowered his huge, muscular body into a kitchen chair.

Like any other wage-earner who has just struggled out of bed, his thoughts were on the day's work ahead. And for 35-year-old Chuck Bednarik—occupation: professional football player—this was to be the most important workday of his life.

In less than five hours—at 12 noon—Bednarik and his Philadelphia Eagle teammates would face the Green Bay Packers in the National Football League championship game at Franklin Field. Eleven years had passed since the Eagles had last played in an NFL title game. Bednarik, then a rookie center, had seen only limited action as the Eagles blanked the Los Angeles Rams, 14-0. But today he expected to spend considerably more time on the field than on the bench.

Bednarik had joined the Eagles as a center in 1949 after twice gaining All-America honors at the University of Pennsylvania and winning the Maxwell Trophy as the nation's outstanding college football player. He switched to linebacker in his second year with the Eagles, and was an All-Pro at that position seven times before moving back to center in 1958.

Now, at an age when most pro football players considered retirement, Chuck Bednarik was seeing more combat than any player in the NFL. In the Eagles' march to the 1960 Eastern Division championship, Bednarik had been called upon to play center on offense and linebacker on defense in several games.

This rare double duty had started in the Eagles' fifth game of the season against the Browns at Cleveland. On the first scrimmage play, Philadelphia linebacker Bob Pellegrini pulled a groin muscle. The spare linebacker, John Nocero, had already been injured in an earlier game. Head coach Buck Shaw summoned Bednarik and said, "Get in there for Pellegrini, Chuck, but don't pull any hero stuff."

That Cleveland game still stood out in Bednarik's mind. Cleveland's Gene Nagler had flattened him with a perfect block from the blind side in the second period. When Chuck staggered to his feet near the Browns' bench, Cleveland coach Paul Brown was clapping his hands. "Now we're playing football," Brown had said.

In the brutal NFL battles between Philadelphia and Cleveland, the Browns had been accused of offering a bounty to the man who "got" Bednarik. This didn't help Chuck's feelings as he tried to shake off the effects of Nagler's ear-ringing block. "I was mad," he said. "I got the idea Paul Brown was making fun of me because I was an old man trying to play two positions. Right then I started playing twice as hard."

Sparked by Bednarik's yeoman work on offense and defense, the Eagles had rallied in the second half to beat the Browns, 31-29. Chuck doubled up in two more games against the New York Giants on successive weekends later in the season. In both games the Eagles came from behind to win, clinching their berth in the championship playoffs. By this time, even Paul Brown had stopped poking fun at

"Old Man" Bednarik. "Chuck is a great two-way player," Brown said. "He's truly amazing."

Bednarik sat by himself in the kitchen, thinking about the rough day ahead of him. By the time his wife and daughters had come downstairs to join him, he had drunk six cups of coffee.

At 9:30 A.M., Bednarik picked up a neighborhood friend in the family car and headed for Franklin Field. On the way, he munched on a chocolate bar. "I can't digest anything else before a game," he explained to the friend. "I'm too tense."

The comment seemed a strange admission from a man who had flown thirty combat missions over Germany as a waist gunner in a B-24 during World War II and now was completing his twelfth season in the NFL. But Bednarik wasn't alone in his reaction. As he entered the Eagle locker room, he greeted quarterback Norm Van Brocklin, another battle-scarred veteran.

"How do you feel, Dutch?" Bednarik asked. Van Brocklin managed a weak smile. "Not so hot," he answered. "This pressure gets worse as you get older." Bednarik nodded in agreement.

As he stripped off his street clothes and climbed into his uniform, Bednarik wondered if the Packers were experiencing the same queasy feeling. "They're probably as nervous as we are," he commented to Van Brocklin.

"I hope so," Van Brocklin replied.

Bednarik (60) talks football with his counterpart, Green Bay center Jim Ringo.

Bednarik's thoughts then drifted to the possible strategy Green Bay would employ. Coached by Vince Lombardi, the Packers had won the Western Division title with an attack built around the power running of fullback Jim Taylor and halfback Paul Hornung.

"They probably won't show us anything new," Bednarik said as he and Van Brocklin trotted onto the field. "If we can stop Taylor and Hornung, we'll win." Van Brocklin winked at the veteran lineman with the dented nose, whacked him across the back and said, "Well, let's go beat 'em, Chuck."

There was an overflow crowd of 67,352 on hand at

kickoff time. The weather was clear, the sun was bright and the temperature stood at forty-eight degrees, unseasonably warm for Philadelphia in late December.

The Eagles won the toss and elected to receive. Timmy Brown ran the kickoff back to the Philadelphia 22. Now it was time for Bednarik and Van Brocklin to go to work. On the first play, Van Brocklin took Bednarik's snap from center and arched a screen pass to Bill Barnes, the left halfback. It was too high. The ball bounced off Barnes's hands and into the arms of Bill Quinlan, Green Bay's defensive right end, who was tackled on the Eagle 15.

Bednarik uttered a silent oath. "What a way to start," he grumbled, shaking his large head. Eleven Green Bay players hurried off the field and eleven new ones came on. Ten Philadelphia players ran off, leaving behind the big man with Number 60 on his green jersey.

Chuck Bednarik, the Eagle center on offense, was now the Eagle left linebacker on defense. He was ready for another iron-man stunt.

Taylor carried first for the Packers, churning through right tackle for 5 yards before Bednarik brought him down. Three more Green Bay running plays—two by Hornung, one by Taylor—failed to gain a first down and the Eagles took over on their own 6-yard line.

The Eagles and their fans were just shaking off the effects of the scare when Green Bay's Bill Forrester recovered a Philadelphia fumble on the Eagles' 20. But the Philadelphia defense, led by the redoubtable Bednarik, again tightened. The Packers had to settle for a 20-yard field goal by Hornung.

In the second period, Hornung booted another field goal and the Packers were ahead, 6-0. With seven minutes left to play in the first half, the Eagles had the ball on their own 35. Tommy McDonald, Philadelphia's excellent little pass catcher, told Van Brocklin in the huddle that he was confident he could beat his man. "He's waiting for me to cut in," McDonald said. "If I can cut out, I'll be free." Van Brocklin nodded. "Okay," he said. "Let's try it."

The play depended on the blocking of Bednarik. After snapping the ball to Van Brocklin, he had to drop back fast to block anyone who broke past the Philadelphia front line. "Someone came through—I didn't see his number—and I knocked him down," Bednarik said later.

The old pro had done his job well. Given this extra time to break loose, McDonald latched onto a perfect lead pass from Van Brocklin and carried it to the Green Bay 35. On the next play, Van Brocklin passed again to McDonald, who caught the ball on the 7 and dashed into the end zone. Bobby Walston added the extra point and later booted a 15-yard field goal. The Eagles left the field at halftime with a 10-6 lead.

Midway through the third period, Green Bay

marched to the Eagle 26-yard line. On third down, the Packers needed 2 yards for a first down.

"In this situation I expected a running play," Bednarik said. "I thought they might send Taylor through the middle, so I tightened up a bit. I positioned myself inside their right end. But the ball went to Hornung and he started toward his right— my zone.

"I remembered from watching some Green Bay films that Hornung liked to cut back on this play, so I was ready for him. Just as he pivoted, I rammed into him. My shoulder dug into his right side under his arm. He went down like a shot. His right arm was quivering. I was really scared."

Bednarik had a reason to be scared. Earlier in the season he had cut down Frank Gifford of the Giants with a similar tackle—vicious, but clean—and Gifford wound up in a hospital with a severe concussion.

Now Hornung was lying there on the soggy Franklin Field turf with big Number 60 hovering over him, a look of sorrow on his face. "I was praying that Paul wasn't seriously injured," he said. Fortunately the Green Bay star had only pinched a nerve in his shoulder. Although he had to leave the game, he was able to return to action later.

The Packers finally scored their first touchdown in the opening minutes of the final quarter on a 7-yard pass from Bart Starr to Max McGee. That put the Lombardi men in front again, 13-10. Phila-

Bednarik's crunching tackle almost forces the ball from Packer halfback Paul Hornung (5).

delphia, though, retaliated quickly. Ted Dean took
the kickoff on the 3-yard line and raced it back to
Green Bay's 39, where Willie Wood fought off two
blockers before knocking Dean out of bounds. Dean
and Bill Barnes then took turns carrying the ball to
the Packer 5-yard line. The Green Bay defenders
dug in for a goal-line stand.

In the Philadelphia huddle, Bednarik winced
when Van Brocklin called a play that would send
Dean on a sweep to the left. "I had a difficult assign-
ment—one of the most difficult for a center," Chuck
said. "I had to snap the ball, then move out to the
left and block their tackle, Henry Jordan, toward
the inside."

Bednarik nailed Jordan with a good block. Another block by Gerry Huth got Dean around the
corner and into the end zone. The Eagles were back
on top, 17-13. By now, Bednarik's body was aching
from the double pounding he had taken on offense
and defense. But he managed to contribute two
more key plays in the remaining minutes. He blunted
Green Bay's next drive by recovering a McGee fumble on Philadelphia's 48.

Then, with fifteen seconds left to play and Green
Bay on the Eagle 20-yard line, Bednarik dropped
back to protect against the pass. Starr couldn't find
a free deep receiver so he threw short to Taylor.

"I was on the 2 when Taylor caught the pass," Bednarik said. "I saw Maxie Baughan bounce off Taylor
at the 15. I moved up. Then Don Burroughs bounced

Happy heroes—quarterback Van Brocklin, Coach Shaw and Bednarik—celebrate in the Eagle locker room.

off Taylor at the 13. I was now on the 9. I set myself. I didn't want Taylor to sidestep me.

"We collided at the 9. I hit him high and put a bear hug around him. Finally Taylor toppled to the ground, his legs still moving. I fell on top, still hugging him. I could see the clock. I saw the second hand sweep past zero. Then I stood up. 'Okay, Taylor,' I said. 'You can get up now. This game is over.'"

And so it was. The Eagles had held on to win, 17-13. The tireless Chuck Bednarik had played fifty-eight of the sixty minutes, taking time out to catch his breath only on kickoffs and punts.

Buck Shaw was certain the Eagles never would have beaten Green Bay without Number 60. "We've got to thank the old pro, Chuck Bednarik, for this one," said the Philadelphia coach. "He held us together on offense and defense. It was an amazing performance by an amazing athlete."

3/Gale Force

CHICAGO: December 12, 1965—Crusty old George Halas, founder, owner and coach of the Chicago Bears, poked his foot into the soggy turf of Wrigley Field an hour before the Bears were to meet the visiting San Francisco Forty-Niners. Halas snorted with disgust. The rain that had fallen all night continued to come down and had made the footing on the field treacherous. "Get the nylon cleats," the Bear coach said to an attendant. "They grip better in this stuff."

Back in the warmth of the Chicago locker room, rookie halfback Gale Sayers, the talk of the National Football League for his brilliant running in recent weeks, quietly changed from rubber cleats to the nylon ones, which were one quarter of an inch longer. Other players chattered nervously, but Sayers didn't say a word. He seldom did.

"He's a shy guy," said offensive guard Mike Rabold, who opened many of the holes that Gale ran through. "You'd never know he's around."

But beneath his placid exterior on this rainy, unusually warm Sunday in December, Gale Sayers was readying himself for the blows and bruises to come. The 200-pound halfback knew that the Forty-Niners would concentrate their defenses on him. Ever since Gale's debut as a starter in the Bears' fourth game of the season, other NFL teams had been learning that they must stop Sayers if they wanted to stop the Bears.

Gale Sayers was used to this kind of special attention. As a track and football star at Omaha Central High School in Omaha, Nebraska, he had had a choice of almost a hundred college scholarship offers. He chose the University of Kansas. After a three-year varsity career in which he rushed for 2,675 yards and became an All-America halfback, he encountered another kind of attention. Two leagues wanted him. He had to make a choice between the Kansas City Chiefs of the American Football League and the Chicago Bears in the rival NFL. He signed with the Bears for an estimated $150,000, three-year contract.

Halas wisely let his prize rookie break in slowly, playing him only briefly in the first two games of the season. Thereafter, Gale began to make himself known. He scored two touchdowns in the third game. The next week, in his first starting role, he produced another touchdown. In the fifth game, he firmly established himself as a regular in Chicago. In a wild 45-37 victory over the Minnesota Vikings,

Sayers scored four touchdowns. This was only two less than the NFL record for touchdowns in a single game—a record held jointly by Ernie Nevers of the old Chicago Cardinals and Dub Jones of the Cleveland Browns.

The flash from Kansas was obviously no flash in the pan. The Bears won eight straight games with him in the starting lineup—after having lost the first three games while Sayers was still adjusting to pro ball. Already Gale had scored sixteen touchdowns, just four less than the NFL record for a season held by Lenny Moore, the great Baltimore Colt runner.

But today he would have to run on a soggy field, a factor that normally should neutralize any good running back's talent.

The Forty-Niners, of course, were not at all unhappy about the mud and rain. They figured the slippery field would cut down Sayers' lightning speed—9.7 seconds for 100 yards—and also deprive him of some of the fantastic cuts and moves he threw at baffled defenders. If he tried to be too fancy or move too quickly, they reasoned, he just might fall on his face.

Sayers had a surprise for the pros, though, who had yet to see him operate under such conditions. As he said later: "I cut on my heels. That helps me keep my footing in the mud. Most backs cut on the balls of their feet."

Proof that Sayers was not like most backs—if

proof were needed—came on the very first play from scrimmage when he took a handoff from quarterback Rudy Bukich and raced 17 yards through the muck for a first down. If the mud had slowed him down, or made him abandon his slick cuts and moves, it certainly wasn't evident on that run. Nor was it evident two minutes later when, after an exchange of punts, the incredible Chicago back took a screen pass from Bukich and started upfield. Because there were so many defenders around him, the play didn't seem as if it would be a long gainer. But with Sayers carrying the ball, no one could be sure.

Gale wiggled. He squirmed. He cut one way, then another. And all the time he maneuvered through the line and linebackers, he was also watching for an opening. He ran easily, using his interference perfectly, waiting for the moment to break. Suddenly he got a big block from guard Jim Cadile, then more blocks from fullback Ronnie Bull and center Mike Pyle. For just an instant Sayers spotted a ray of daylight through the mass of San Francisco tacklers trying to bring him down.

Boom! Sayers took two incredibly quick lateral steps that got him past a trio of onrushing Forty-Niner defenders. Then with a smooth change of gears from cruising speed to full throttle, he hurtled into the clear. As he crossed the last stripe to complete an 80-yard touchdown run, Sayers handed the ball to the official. Gale was expressionless as

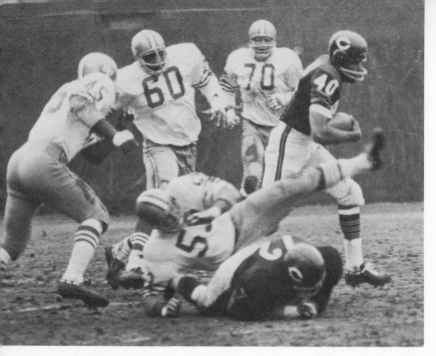

Sayers (40) leaves his Forty-Niner opponents befuddled.

usual. The Forty-Niners, however, were open-mouthed. Later, defensive back El Kimbrough, one of Sayers' victims on the play, said: "He's just great. You're hesitant to commit yourself against him. But if you lay back . . . well, you can't do that either."

Naturally, the crowd of 46,278 Bear fans at Wrigley Field appreciated Sayers' artistry far more than the Forty-Niners did. Though they had no way of knowing it at the time, Gale's 80-yard burst was just the start of an unforgettable afternoon for the magnificent back.

There were five minutes remaining in the second quarter and the Bears were ahead, 13-7, when Gale swept around left end with a handoff. He stayed in cruising speed until Rabold and Cadile chopped a hole in the Forty-Niner wall in front of him. Then he zoomed into passing gear and popped through the hole for a 21-yard touchdown run. As the first half came to an end, Sayers virtually repeated the play from 7 yards out. It was his third touchdown of the afternoon and nineteenth of the season, just one less than Lenny Moore's record total. During his 7-yard scoring run, Gale uttered the only words that anyone on the field heard from him all day.

"He patted my bottom," recalled Rabold, who was out in front blocking, "and said, 'Keep going.'"

Actually, Gale did not have to do much talking on this day. Others were doing his talking for him. "I wish I had the vocabulary to describe him," said John David Crow, San Francisco's veteran fullback, a man not known to be generous with praise. "He's a great, great football player already, at a very young age. He has quickness and speed, but he has something else that a great back must have. He has a sense of football, a feel for the game. It's easy for a coach to tell a back, 'Follow your guard around end and then make your move.' But there is more to it than that. You have to see downfield, and Sayers must see an awful lot to make the runs he does."

Soon the halftime intermission was over and the teams were back for the start of the third quarter. With just 3:50 gone in the third quarter, Sayers took a pitchout from Bukich at midfield. Spotting an opening right away, he turned on his searing

In an open field, Sayers is untouchable.

speed and simply outran everyone to the end zone for his fourth touchdown.

Late in the third quarter, Sayers had a chance to demonstrate still another of his many skills as a runner—raw, bone-crunching power. On fourth down from the Forty-Niner 1-yard line, Gale took a handoff and blasted straight ahead, jack-knifing over the goal line and knocking bigger men back with the force of his drive. It was touchdown number five of the game and number twenty of the season. He had tied the NFL record for touchdowns in a season and was just one away from the single-game mark.

The crowd went wild, screaming over and over, "We want Sayers." But with the Bears leading, 40-13, Halas wasn't about to risk his star's health. He decided Sayers would not carry the ball from scrimmage again. If he was to tie the record, it would have to be accomplished while returning a punt or kickoff.

The game moved on toward its end and, as time passed and Sayers remained on the bench, the crowd began to lose hope of seeing a record-tying sixth touchdown in one game. But they were giving up too soon for, with eight minutes gone in the final period, the San Franciscans had to punt from their own 43-yard line. A hush fell over Wrigley Field as Sayers stood on his 15, barely visible through the fog, rain and oncoming dusk. Tommy Davis punted and the ball sailed down to Sayers. Now eleven frus-

Gale makes headway through a crowd of Forty-Niners

for one of his record touchdowns.

trated San Francisco tacklers were determined, on one play, to make up for a whole afternoon of humiliation.

Gary Lewis, a block of a man at 230 pounds, had the first chance to tackle Sayers, who caught the ball on one of the mushiest portions of the field. "I had a good shot at him," Lewis said. "I knew he'd be going to his right to get out of that soggy patch and over to dry land and I was in good position to stop him. I don't know why I missed him except that he's a heck of a back and lots of others had shots, too, and missed him."

Lots of others? It looked as though each of the Forty-Niners had a shot at him. After Lewis missed, Sayers roared straight up the field, right at a nest of San Francisco defenders. But at the last possible moment, he sidestepped the mass of players, buzzing right by all of them. Ken Willard, another 230-pounder, came closest to downing the flying Chicago star, but not close enough.

"He faked me out of my pants," Willard later admitted. "He makes such deceptive moves at full speed that you have to try to keep moving with him. You can't get set and wait for him to run to you."

Breaking past the initial wave of tacklers, Sayers swerved to his left, forcing the remaining defenders to move in that direction. Then he somehow cut back against the flow of motion—all without breaking stride. It was the classic move of a classic back. Before the startled Forty-Niners could reverse their field, Gale was on his way to the end zone.

"He doesn't look much different from other backs until he turns on his real quick moves," said San Francisco defensive back George Donnelly. "He moves laterally as fast as he does straight away."

The sixth touchdown, which covered 85 yards, made even the unemotional Sayers lose his cool for a moment. After his first five scores, Gale had just handed the ball to the nearest referee. But after the sixth, which tied the single-game record and gave him a total of 22 touchdowns for the year, he flipped the ball into the air, clapped his hands, skipped back toward his teammates on the field and then sprinted to the bench. Minutes later the gun went off. The final score: Chicago 61, San Francisco 20.

As the winners jubilantly sprinted toward their locker room, old George Halas saw Sayers flash by and said, "That was the greatest game of football I have ever seen a man play."

4/The First Super Bowl

LOS ANGELES: January 15, 1967—The sun shone through the typical California haze as 61,946 football fans sat in the mammoth Los Angeles Coliseum, awaiting the start of the game they and millions more had eagerly anticipated for years.

The Super Bowl—or the AFL–NFL World Championship Game as pro football officials christened it—had finally arrived, and in a few hours either the Kansas City Chiefs or the Green Bay Packers would be the world champions of pro football.

For the owners in both leagues, there must have been a sigh of relief after all the tumultuous events leading to the first Super Bowl. These had included an angry battle of words and money, dating all the way back to the formation of the American Football League in 1959.

The AFL had had its beginnings when two Texas oil millionaires, Lamar Hunt and K. S. "Bud"

Adams, decided to form a new league to rival the entrenched, 39-year-old National Football League. Hunt and Adams found six other individuals who were interested in owning teams, and the AFL began play in 1960. At first its progress was slow, but as the league became more established, it started upping its bids for the top college players. The New York Jets paid over $600,000 for two quarterbacks, Joe Namath and John Huarte, in 1965. The following year the Green Bay Packers of the NFL retaliated by spending about one million dollars for Donny Anderson and Jim Grabowski. Some players who couldn't even make the teams were getting bonuses up to $100,000.

Obviously, there was a limit to how far this reckless competition could go. And the only way to solve the situation was for the leagues to merge. The heated rivals joined together in the spring of 1966.

From the fans' standpoint, the main feature of the merger was the Super Bowl game.

As more than 60,000 fans, including ten astronauts, moved into the Coliseum and found their seats, they eagerly awaited the moment when the Green Bay Packers, champions of the established NFL, would take the field against the Kansas City Chiefs, champions of the upstart AFL.

The opponents had earned their trips to Los Angeles two weeks earlier by winning their league title contests. Green Bay had defeated the Dallas

Cowboys, 34-27, and Kansas City had walloped the Buffalo Bills, 31-7.

The winners then took a few days off before flying to the West Coast. While two television networks then reminded everyone that this was Super Week, the Chiefs and the Packers were working out near Los Angeles.

At the Chiefs' base in Long Beach, cornerback Fred Williamson had quickly become the center of attention when he started telling anyone who was interested how he intended to use his "hammer" against the Packers. "Before the game, they'll think that a hammer is just an instrument used to drive a nail into a board," Williamson had said. "But by Sunday night, they'll have an entirely different definition."

Williamson's hammer closely resembled a karate chop which he delivered at a receiver just after the opponent caught a pass. "I prefer a perpendicular chop on the top of the helmet," he boasted. "They remember that more, and it gives them something to think about when they line up on my side the next time."

Other Chiefs, however, had talked more soberly about the game and the significance it held. After all, there was a $15,000 prize for each member of the winning team and $7,500 for each loser.

For example, Jim Tyrer, Kansas City's 292-pound offensive tackle, had said: "I'm excited about it, not just about representing Jim Tyrer, or the Chiefs, but the whole league and everybody who's had anything to do with it. It's been a long fight, and not all of it's been fun. But here, on one day, we have a chance to get what we've wanted for seven years—recognition."

Hank Stram, the Kansas City coach, agreed. "It's been a war of words for seven years," he said, "and now we'll settle it on the grass."

About 120 miles to the north, in Santa Barbara, the Packers had no thought of taking the Chiefs lightly just because they were representing what all NFL people felt was an inferior league. "To lose," safetyman Willie Wood said, "would be to wipe out everything we've tried to do this season. We've won the NFL championship again, but if we don't win this one, what good is it?"

This, of course, was the game to win, and the Packers were heavily favored to do so.

As the six officials, three from each league, got into position, Kansas City's kicking team and Green Bay's receiving squad trotted onto the field.

Moments later Fletcher Smith's kickoff floated down to the Green Bay 5-yard line, Herb Adderley gathered it in and the world championship game was under way. Adderley brought the kick back to his own 25. Three plays later the Packers had their initial first down as Jim Taylor ran for 7 yards on two plays and Elijah Pitts gained 5 on another. The first down looked easy.

Just as quickly, however, Bart Starr ran into trou-

Quarterback Bart Starr tries to lift a pass

over the charging Chiefs.

ble. An eleven-year veteran from Alabama, he was the engineer of the Lombardi locomotive, and many had expected the game to revolve around him. But Starr's first pass, intended for Max McGee, fell incomplete. McGee had just replaced Boyd Dowler, who had reinjured his right shoulder on the third play of the game. Starr dropped back to pass on second down, too, but this time he never got it off. Instead, 6-foot 7-inch Buck Buchanan smashed past the Packer linemen and threw Starr down at the 27 for a 10-yard loss. Starr was smothered again on the next play.

The I-told-you-sos suddenly turned into maybe-we-better-wait-and-sees. The Packers had been the heavy favorites, but the Chiefs had shown in less than a minute that they weren't about to become sacrificial lambs.

The Chiefs got even more of a lift when they, too, made a first down in three plays. But then, like the Packers, they had to punt four plays later.

After Green Bay's Pitts, playing for the injured Paul Hornung, swung around right end for 3 yards, Starr connected with tight end Marv Fleming for 11 yards and with Pitts for 22 more, placing the ball in Kansas City's territory for the first time, at the 44. Taylor, the burly fullback, lost 5 yards on first down, but Starr came right back with a 12-yard completion to Carroll Dale, making it third and 3 at the Chiefs' 37.

Now the always cool Starr faded back, looking for

the crucial first down. He saw McGee heading down-field, but he also saw safety Bobby Hunt start moving over to help cornerback Willie Mitchell cover McGee. The quarterback threw the ball, but he put it a little behind his receiver to make sure there wouldn't be an interception. McGee reached back with his right hand, grabbed the ball, scooped it under his arm as he crossed the 20. Without breaking stride, McGee raced the rest of the way for the first score of the game. Don Chandler kicked the extra point, and the predominantly NFL crowd roared its approval of Green Bay's 7-0 lead.

If the Chiefs were to keep the game close, they would have to strike back with a quick score. They threatened to do just that following the kickoff, marching to the Packer 33. But the drive stalled. So did a field goal try.

The Chiefs, however, stopped Green Bay again in their next drive. Len Dawson, an AFL star who had failed in the older league, was determined to take the Chiefs all the way to a touchdown. He started by eluding the hard-charging Packer line and flipping a screen pass to rookie Mike Garrett, who broke three tackles and slipped swiftly through the Green Bay defense for 17 yards.

The veteran quarterback then switched to the ground, handing to Bert Coan for 3 yards, Curtis McClinton for 6 and Coan again for 2 more and a first down at the Packer 38. Now Dawson returned to the air, faking another handoff before racing to

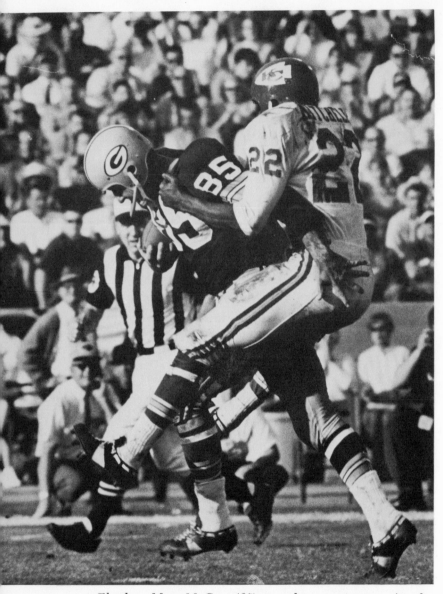

Flanker Max McGee (85) caught more passes in the Super Bowl game than he did in the whole season.

his left and spotting Otis Taylor at the 13. Taylor, one of the most adept pass catchers in the league, pulled down the ball and raced to the 7 before the Green Bay safety, Tom Brown, pulled him down.

Just 7 yards away from the tie, the Chiefs appeared to turn conservative. Dawson started to hand the ball off for a try at the Packer line. Instead he pulled the ball back and looked for receivers. McClinton and split end Chris Burford both floated into the left corner of the end zone with only Willie Wood to cover the two of them.

As soon as Wood broke toward Burford, Dawson fired to McClinton for the score. Mercer added the extra point, and with 4:20 gone in the second period, the Super Bowl was tied, 7-7.

The Packers needed only three plays to get into the end zone again, but Starr's 64-yard scoring pass to Dale was wiped out when one of the officials called Bob Skoronski, the Packer left tackle, for illegal procedure. Undaunted, Starr returned to the methodical attack with which the Packers had worn down opponents all season. Effectively mixing his plays, Starr moved the Packers steadily downfield, completing a toss to McGee for 10 yards, a second to Dale for 15 and one to Fleming for 11. That brought the ball to the Kansas City 27. There the drive seemed to stall as the Packers got only three yards on two running plays.

But on third down, with 7 yards to go for a first down, Starr threw to Pitts for 10 yards to the Chiefs'

14. The wily quarterback then pitched back to Taylor, who swept around left end behind the blocking of guards Jerry Kramer and Fuzzy Thurston. Taylor rambled into the end zone for the second Packer touchdown. The Packers led, 14-7.

On the first play after the kickoff, Packer defensive end Lionel Aldridge and tackle Henry Jordan dropped Dawson for an 8-yard loss. But Dawson was not to be intimidated by the hard rush. He promptly connected with tight end Fred Arbanas for 12 yards, Taylor for 11 and Burford for 27, and Kansas City was back at Green Bay's 32.

But the drive fizzled and Mercer was called on to try another field goal. This time he was right on target from the 31, and the Chiefs had cut the deficit to 14-10.

The fans couldn't hide their surprise at the unexpectedly tough fight the underdog Chiefs were giving the NFL kings in the first half. In fact, Kansas City compiled the more impressive statistics, outgaining the Packers 181 yards to 164.

In the Packer locker room, meanwhile, Vince Lombardi—the master thinker, the master tactician, the master winner—was admonishing his team for what he thought they had done wrong in the first half. "Stop grabbing and start tackling," Lombardi told his players. "Be more aggressive."

In the other locker room, Hank Stram told his players to keep playing the way they had been. "We can win it," he said.

Halfback Donny Anderson (44) barges through two Chiefs for extra yardage.

Dawson opened the second half by scrambling around right end for 15 yards and a first down. After two more runs, Dawson dropped back to pass, trying to get the Chiefs into Green Bay territory once again. Immediately, he saw that the Packer linebackers were blitzing. Dave Robinson rushed in from the left and Lee Roy Caffey stormed in from the right. At the same time Arbanas was throwing a head fake at Wood, the free safety, and cutting toward the sideline where he expected the ball to be. The pass never made it. Caffey's upraised hand just nicked the ball, and the pass wobbled short of its mark. Wood cut in front of Arbanas, intercepted the ball at his own 45 and broke down the sideline.

Fifty yards later, Garrett caught up with Wood and dragged him down from behind. But the Packers had the ball at the 5 and Pitts needed only one try to slice through left tackle behind Skoronski for Green Bay's third touchdown and a 21-10 lead.

While many of the fans expected the Chiefs to give up, the American Leaguers had no such inclination. They got one first down and looked as if they were going to get another in Packer territory, but Caffey knifed through on third down and tackled Coan for a 4-yard loss. Kansas City punted.

The Chiefs got the ball back three minutes later, and Dawson immediately went to the air. His first pass, to Burford, was incomplete.

As Dawson faded back, on second down, 250-pound Caffey and 245-pound Willie Davis smashed through the Chiefs' pass protection and smothered Dawson for a 14-yard loss. Shrugging off the double jolt, Dawson started back again on third down and this time suffered a triple jolt as Davis, 250-pound Jordan and 260-pound Ron Kostelnik buried him at his own 2. At this point Dawson gladly gave way to punter Jerrel Wilson.

The Packer defensive's success seemed to rub off on the offense as Starr got the Packer attack moving once again. He passed to McGee for 11 yards and four plays later found McGee open again on the right side of the Chiefs' secondary for a 16-yard gain to Kansas City's 28.

Two more plays went by before Starr sent McGee down past cornerback Mitchell again, and the 34-year-old Texan made a juggling catch for his sixth reception and second touchdown of the day. The play covered 13 yards, and after Chandler's fourth conversion, the score was Green Bay 28, Kansas City 10.

In the fourth quarter, Dawson tried to put the ball in the air, but Kansas City held the ball for just 62 seconds before having to give it up again. They got it back just as quickly, though, when Mitchell intercepted another Starr to McGee aerial. It was the first time Starr had been intercepted in 173 passes, dating back to October 16, 1966, in Chicago.

Suddenly and dramatically, the Chiefs came to life. Dawson fired to McClinton, who made a diving catch for a 27-yard gain. The determined quarter-

Commissioner Pete Rozelle, left, presents football's greatest trophy to Packer Coach Vince Lombardi.

back then hit Taylor for 4 yards and Burford for 12 to the Green Bay 46. That was as far as the Chiefs got. Dawson was knocked down by Davis for a 10-yard loss, then threw two errant passes.

The ball went over to Green Bay and Starr wasted no time manipulating the discouraged Chiefs. He completed another pass to McGee, giving the veteran seven catches for 138 yards, more than he accumulated in the 14-game regular season. Soon after, Pitts tallied Green Bay's fifth touchdown on a 1-yard burst around the left side.

Green Bay finished the game well in front, 35-10.

Lombardi was reluctant to make any boasts about

NFL superiority. But wave after wave of reporters pressed him until he finally said: "In my opinion the Chiefs don't rate with the top teams in the National Football League. They're a good football team with fine speed, but I'd have to say NFL football is tougher."

The American Football League would have to wait for another day and another Super Bowl to prove otherwise.

5/Jim Brown's Repeat Performance

CLEVELAND: November 19, 1961—Nine minutes into the opening period, Bobby Walston booted a 34-yard field goal to give the Philadelphia Eagles a 3-0 lead over the Cleveland Browns. A victory for the Eagles would move them closer to the first-place New York Giants and the Browns would be dumped deeper into third place.

So there were actually two games going on in Cleveland's Municipal Stadium: the Browns-Eagles game on the field, and the Giants-Pittsburgh Steelers game on the scoreboard. But Jim Brown's eyes did not glance up at the huge scoreboard. They remained fixed hard on the field of play, growing more intense as they watched Walston's field goal split the uprights. A moment later, the Eagle kickoff was returned to the Browns' 21-yard line and Cleveland's Jim Brown shucked off his parka, adjusted the chin strap of his orange helmet and went to work.

During his four and a half seasons in the National Football League, Jim had been rewriting the record

Jim Brown leaves the Eagles grounded.

book at as fast and furious a pace as the way he ran
when he had a football in his hands. His powerful
fullback smashes into the line bowled over 260-
pound defensive linemen, outbulled tough linebackers and slammed past fleet halfbacks. Once in the
open, he was uncatchable.

Jim Brown came into the NFL after a career as
an outstanding all-around schoolboy athlete at
Manhasset High on New York's Long Island, and
as an All-America at Syracuse University. He had
come to Long Island by way of Georgia, where he
was born on St. Simons Island. His mother had gone
north to seek better employment after Jim's father
left home. She left him with his great-grandmother,
whom he called "Mama." But Mama always told
him, "Someday your mother will send for you."

When he was eight, Jim's mother did send for
him. She had a job as a maid for a family in Great
Neck, an exclusively white, affluent community
in Long Island. Jim began attending school a few
miles away in Manhasset, which was somewhat more
mixed racially and considerably less affluent than
Great Neck. After Jim was too big to share his
mother's one-room apartment, he roomed with a
Negro family in Manhasset.

He began to discover his natural athletic talents
while attending Manhasset High School. Before
coming north, Jim Brown had never seen a football
game. On Long Island he watched boys his age
playing football on sandlots picked clean of rocks

and broken glass. He began to learn the game and before long was the best athlete at Manhasset High, outshining all others in football, basketball, track and lacrosse. Teachers and other adults began to show an interest in Jim and urged him to pursue a career in sports. Even then, Ed Walsh, his football coach at Manhasset High, told him: "You can be a professional football player. But you've got to go to college first. And you won't get to college unless you start taking your studies seriously."

Jim began to pay more attention to his schoolwork. But he didn't stop hustling on the playing field. During his four years as a halfback on the football team, he averaged nearly 15 yards a carry, and Manhasset lost only two of its games. In basketball, the 6-foot 1-inch Brown once set a Long Island high school record by scoring 53 points in a single game. He then broke his own mark the following week with 55 points. In his senior year he averaged 38 points a game. He was also a star on the lacrosse team.

By graduation time, Jim, now nearly full grown, had received scholarship offers from 45 colleges. He selected Syracuse on the advice of a close friend, Kenneth Molloy. Molloy, an attorney and a Syracuse alumnus, told Jim that Syracuse was embarking on a big-time schedule and would become a national power within a few short years.

So Jim Brown entered Syracuse in the fall of 1953. The only Negro on the squad, Jim took most of his sophomore season to earn a starter's job. After that, Jim Brown and Syracuse were on their way together—up the football ladder. As a junior, he finished second in the East in rushing yardage. In his senior year he scored 43 points against arch-rival Colgate. While winning games over tougher opponents, he rolled up 125 yards against Army and 145 yards against Maryland.

Syracuse lost only one game in Jim's senior year and received a bid to play in the New Year's Day Cotton Bowl game against Texas Christian. Even though the Orangemen lost, 28-27, Jim was thrust into the national spotlight for the first time. With millions watching him on television, Jim scored twenty-one of Syracuse's twenty-seven points and was named the game's outstanding player. He had become a celebrity.

The Cleveland Browns drafted Jim and almost immediately began comparing him to Marion Mot-ley. Motley was regarded as the greatest fullback in the Browns' history. Now 6 feet 2 inches and weighing 220 pounds, Jim was switched from half-back to fullback by Paul Brown, coach and founder of the team that bore his name.

In his rookie year, Jim led all of the league's runners in rushing with 942 yards. Against the Los Angeles Rams alone, he set a one-game record by going 237 yards. He was named Rookie of the Year, and the Browns won the Eastern Conference title.

In 1958 the Browns slid to second place, but

Jimmy won the rushing title again with a record 1,527 yards. He also topped the league with eighteen touchdowns and 108 points. The following year, in a game against the Baltimore Colts, Jim scored five touchdowns, including a 70-yarder, to lead the Browns to a 38-31 victory. He again led the NFL rushers with 1,329 yards and a high of fourteen touchdowns. In 1960, he went 1,257 yards for an unprecedented fourth consecutive rushing title. Four years, four rushing titles. A running back couldn't do better than that.

So here at Cleveland Municipal Stadium Jim Brown was going to work in yet another game. The Browns were hoping for the Eastern crown. And Jim himself was going for a fifth rushing title. Every time he stepped onto the field he was capable of setting some new record. But with the Eagles ahead, 3-0, records weren't on Jim Brown's mind this cold afternoon. He was thinking only of what lay immediately ahead—the next play.

The Browns were unable to score on their next series of downs, though with Jimmy carrying the ball five times they got as far as the Eagle 16-yard line before they were stopped. The next time they got the ball, toward the close of the first quarter, they really began to move. Jimmy Brown took a flare pass from quarterback Milt Plum and rumbled 39 yards to the Eagle 21-yard line just as the period came to an end.

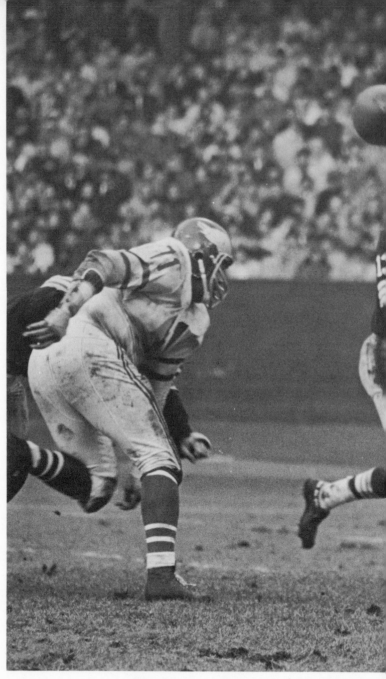

The Browns often used short passes

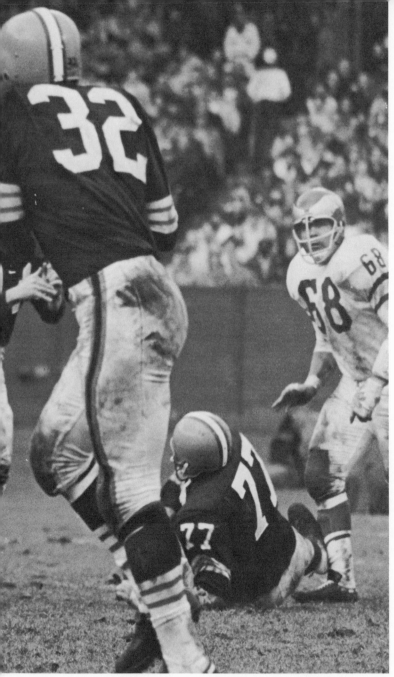

from Frank Ryan (13) to get Jim Brown loose.

After Plum tried a pass that failed, the Browns decided to go with their man Brown again. Jimmy banged the Eagle left side for 18 yards, then smashed through the middle to put the ball on the two. From there, he cracked over for a Cleveland touchdown and Lou Groza's kick put the Browns in front, 7-3.

The Eagles charged back on a 68-yard drive in twelve plays, taking back the lead, 10-7. But shortly before the half ended, the Browns struck again and it was Jimmy Brown who spearheaded the attack. Cleveland took over on its own 17 and went all the way. Jimmy took the football most of the distance, lugging it 40 yards on five carries and a 12-yard pass play.

With the ball down on the 3, the Eagles stacked their line against a Jim Brown smash into the middle. So Jim swept left end for his second score of the day and the Browns led, 14-10. The hometown fans, some 68,399 strong, gave the Browns a roaring ovation as they left the field for halftime. Still, no one was aware of the kind of day this was going to be for Jim Brown.

By the time the Browns returned for the start of the third quarter, the scoreboard at Municipal Stadium showed that the Giants were comfortably ahead of the Steelers. Perhaps first place was out of reach today, but second place was within the grasp of the Browns. All that stood in their way was the Eagles, whom they led by a scant four points.

Jim Brown quickly boosted the Browns' chances.

He took Ted Dean's kickoff on his own three and ran it back to the Brown 27. The ensuing drive lasted only eight plays. With Jimmy running for 13 more yards and blocking ferociously when he wasn't carrying the ball, the Browns moved quickly to the Eagle 28. From there Plum tossed a touchdown pass to Bobby Mitchell. Now the score was 21-10.

Late in the third quarter, the Browns got possession of the ball again. Leading by eleven points, they decided to ride the ball on the ground for a while to eat up time on the clock. That meant it was time for Jim Brown to go to work again. He drove off right tackle for 9 yards. On second down, he slanted off left tackle for 14 more yards and a Cleveland first down at the Eagle 49. Then he split the middle of the Eagle line for 4 yards and it became clear that there would be no stopping him.

He was running, as always, with tremendous drive and balance and fearsome power. Enemy defenders stood in his way, but Jimmy's great strength bowled them over or enabled him to wrestle free from their clutches. On the Cleveland bench, veteran Brown players were trying to recall if they had ever seen Jimmy have a bigger day as a ball-carrier. Even his teammates, however, had no idea of the amount of yardage he was chewing up with his runs. Most unaware of all was Brown himself. The big man with Number 32 on his jersey had no idea how many yards he had gained. And even if he had known, he couldn't have cared less.

Brown scampers to a 13-yard gain against the Eagles.

On the next series of downs, Jim carried the ball four more times for a total of 30 yards to put Cleveland in position for a Groza field goal from 22 yards out. It was now a 24-10 game.

Victory appeared to be out of reach for the Eagles. And the Giants were on their way to defeating the Steelers. Just to be on the safe side, the Browns decided to keep the ball on the ground. So at the beginning of the fourth quarter, it was Jim Brown for 5 yards, then 9 more and a first down. Less than a minute after the start of the period, Jim went over from the 1-yard line for his third touchdown of the day.

Up in the press box at Municipal Stadium, the sportswriters were growing excited. "If he keeps running at this pace," one of them said, "he could break his own rushing record. You know, the one he set against the Rams as a rookie, when he went 237 yards." The final score of the game now became of secondary importance.

The next time the Browns got the ball, Jim went for 16 yards straight up the middle, battering the very heart of the Eagle defense and shaking off tacklers as if they were fleas. He seemed unstoppable now, indestructible. He went for 4 yards, then got a brief rest while Bobby Mitchell swept right end for 11 yards. After that it was Brown for 6, Brown for 13 more and another first down. Three plays later, Jimmy turned the Eagle right end for 8 yards and his fourth touchdown of the game. Municipal Stadium roared its approval. In the press box at the top of the stadium, statisticians were hunched over their charts, adding up figures.

Now Cleveland led, 45-17, with just two minutes to play. Even though the Brown lead was overwhelming, Coach Paul Brown left in his first-stringers. And the ball went to Jimmy Brown on the last few plays. He broke up the middle for 8 yards. He swept his own right end for 4 yards and a first down. Then he went up the middle again for 7 yards. Finally the gun went off, ending the game.

The victorious Browns ran off the field. They were a happy bunch in their locker room. By beating the Eagles they had climbed into second place in the Eastern Conference. The following week they would meet the Giants and see what they could do about first place.

Jim Brown was dropping his equipment to the floor in preparation for his shower when a sportswriter rushed up to him, shouting, "Congratulations!"

"For what?" Brown asked.

"For breaking your own rushing record, of course," the writer said.

Brown's previous record had been 237 yards. In his incredible performance against the Eagles, statisticians had totaled 242 yards—an NFL record.

Jim shrugged. He wasn't impressed. He wasn't being blasé; somehow records had never meant very much to him. In fact, he once said he disliked

Jim accepts congratulations for his record day.

breaking records because it makes people look upon athletes as statistics. This robs them of their individuality and tends to obscure what they really are as athletes.

Later, it was discovered that the statisticians in the press box had been hasty. In rechecking Jim's rushing figures for the day, they found their addition had been wrong. The correct figures showed that Jim had rushed for 237 yards, by coincidence the same number of yards he had gained in his record-setting 1957 game against the Rams.

6/When the Saints Went Marching In

NEW ORLEANS: September 17, 1967—The roar from the crowd of 80,879 reached a fever pitch in Tulane Stadium as the brand-new New Orleans Saints ran onto the field. Trumpeter Al Hirt, a part owner of the new franchise, was tooting "When The Saints Go Marching In" as the National Football League team appeared for its first regular-season game against the Los Angeles Rams.

The festive crowd appreciated the 86-degree weather, the clear skies and the music of Hirt. But most of all the crowd appreciated the Saints, who had surprised the world of pro football with their pre-season performance. The Saints had won five straight exhibition games after losing, 16-7, to the Los Angeles Rams.

"The sound was deafening," said John Gilliam, a rookie running back for the Saints. Gilliam had not played before so many people during an entire college season at little South Carolina State. "When we first came out to warm up, there weren't many

The opening-game program becomes a collector's item for Saint fans.

people in the stands yet. There was only a little applause. But when we came back onto the field just before the start of the game, the crowd had grown and it had really come alive."

Gilliam had survived the rugged training period

in San Diego, California, where Coach Tom Fears had been forced to cut more players than he now carried on his forty-man roster. At the same time, Fears had to establish confidence in the players he wanted to keep.

"There were so many running backs in camp, I didn't know what I was doing there," said Gilliam, the fifty-fourth player selected in the first combined National and American League draft. "I had been primarily a pass receiver in college. But when the Saints drafted me in the second round, they said that I was to be a running back. So I tried to become one."

The Saints' top running backs were supposed to be Jim Taylor and Paul Hornung, the same pair that had led the Green Bay Packers to NFL titles in 1961, 1962, 1965 and 1966. Taylor, who had played out his option with the Packers and had returned to his native state of Louisiana, was on the field ready to go. But Hornung, one of the forty-two players the Saints had drafted from the rest of the NFL, was not there. A pinched nerve had caused him to retire to a coaching role with the Saints.

Both Taylor and Hornung had come to the Saints with big names. Gilliam had come to New Orleans the hard way. He was sixteen years old before he ever played organized football, but he had been averaging 25 points for the Brewer High School basketball team in Greenwood, South Carolina. "The football coach noticed how fast I was getting downcourt and asked me why I didn't come out for the team," Gilliam said. "I thought it would be a waste of time, but as a senior I tried out."

This was his start on the road to pro football. "But I never thought I would end up in New Orleans," John said. "From my sophomore year on at South Carolina State, the Rams were in contact with me. So were seventeen other pro teams before I was drafted, but never the Saints."

The Saints had become the sixteenth NFL entry on November 1, 1966—All-Saints Day—while Gilliam was near the end of his senior season at

Al Hirt, a part-owner of the Saints, cheers his new team on with his famous Dixieland trumpet.

South Carolina State. Gilliam didn't pay much attention to the awarding of the Saint franchise. He was too busy.

Besides going full-time on offense, John was playing safety on the seventh-best small-college defense that year. He also returned kickoffs, three of them for touchdowns. "The best was for 98 yards in the season opener against Florida A&M," John said. "I went all the way and we won, 8-3. It was the only time that we beat them in my three years."

But South Carolina State and Florida A&M seemed light-years away as Gilliam stood on the field before more than 80,000 fans. They were there to support the franchise which had been bought for $8.5 million by a group headed by oilman John Mecom, Jr., who, at 28, was only six years older than Gilliam. Mecom had been named the principal owner in December, 1966. One of his first moves was to hire Vic Schwenk as his director of player personnel. Schwenk had previously been with the Rams, the same team that was facing the Saints in their first regular-season game, the same team which had been in contact with Gilliam for more than two years.

When the Rams ran onto the Sugar Bowl field, the sound of applause was noticeably absent. It was just the opposite of Anaheim, California, on August 2 when the California team had played host to the Saints. Since losing that exhibition game with the Rams, the Saints had gone on to defeat the St.

On the field, quarterback Bill Kilmer (17) leads the young Saints.

Louis Cardinals, Pittsburgh Steelers, San Francisco Forty-Niners, Miami Dolphins and Atlanta Falcons. In the process, they had found a leader in quarterback Bill Kilmer, who had won the starting job over Gary Cuozzo and Gary Wood.

After a thunderous welcome for Taylor, it was game time. The referee, John Pace, signaled that the Saints had come up winners in their first official coin toss. The Saints decided to receive.

Bruce Gossett, the place-kicking champion in the NFL, teed up the football on his 40-yard line, backed off and tried to ignore the noise of the crowd. Some 60 yards away Gilliam stood, listening and waiting. Gossett was anxious to start the game—so anxious that when he kicked the ball he was one step ahead of his teammates.

The ball sailed to Gilliam, and the Saints officially started their first NFL game. Gilliam was on the move as he caught the ball at his own 6-yard line. Controlling the speed which had enabled him to run the 100-yard dash in 9.5 seconds in college, Gilliam headed straight upfield with a wedge of Saints in front of him. Near midfield, he spotted daylight.

"He went right between me and Dave Pivec," said Ram guard Tom Mack. "Neither of us touched him."

Gilliam then angled toward the left sideline, opened up and turned on all his blazing speed. He reached the end zone without being touched.

There, he was mobbed by Saint players. Officially the New Orleans Saints were only fifteen seconds old and already they had a touchdown. No other team in the history of NFL football had ever begun its initial game with a touchdown.

The vocal thunder from the capacity crowd increased. The Saints had scored. John Gilliam had scored. All on the first play in Saint history. It didn't matter that the Rams finally won the game, 27-13. The Saints had truly marched in.

7/Yat's Aerial Circus

NEW YORK: October 28, 1962—The New York Giants were taking the field for their warmup session before the game with the Washington Redskins. As they ran out onto the Yankee Stadium turf, they were led by Number 14, quarterback Y.A. Tittle. The 62,000 spectators found it easy to spot Tittle. He was wearing a red baseball cap. And he was the only player on the field with his head covered during the pre-game drills.

Throughout his professional career Yelberton Abraham Tittle never did look much like a football player. He would come to the field dressed more like a banker, wearing a dark suit, an overcoat and a matching hat. He made the hat a requirement—it covered his bald head.

Even when he was a student at Louisiana State University, Y.A. had worn a hat constantly. In fact, at LSU he picked up the nickname "The Bald Eagle."

Inside that balding head, however, was a football

Tittle goes over game strategy with Coach Allie Sherman.

mind which made Y.A. Tittle one of the great quarterbacks in pro football history. His knowledge of the game was as complete as any quarterback's. This knowledge, plus a burning desire for the game he loved, an overpowering will to win and the ability to hurl a football up to 65 yards in the air, kept Y.A. Tittle in the pros for seventeen seasons.

The first two of those seasons were spent with the Baltimore Colts of the old All-America Conference. When that league disbanded after the 1949 season, Y.A. moved to San Francisco of the National Football League. He was the Forty-Niners' starting quarterback for ten years.

Then Red Hickey, the San Francisco coach, decided to install a new "shotgun" offense in place of the standard "T" formation. Tittle, 34 years old at the time, just wasn't strong enough or quick enough to make the shotgun offense go. Though he loved to run with the ball, Tittle couldn't stand up under the frequent running that Hickey's new formation required. So Hickey traded him to the Giants for a young guard named Lou Cordileone. Cordileone best summed up the feelings of most fans when the trade was announced. "Me for Tittle?" he said. "You mean, just *me?*"

The answer was yes. New York wanted Y.A. as a backup man for aging Charley Conerly. But Giant coach Allie Sherman didn't know Y.A. Tittle personally. Although he knew that Y.A. could still throw the ball, he wasn't aware of the spirit and fire that were still inside the "old man." And he didn't realize just how well Y.A. was going to fit into the Giant style of play.

Sherman soon found out. After only four games of the regular season, Y.A. took over from Conerly as the leading man. He ran most of the show for the rest of the 1961 season and led New York to the division title, completing 163 passes in 285 attempts for 2,272 yards and seventeen touchdowns.

In the game against Washington he was picking up right where he had left off in 1961. Conerly had retired, leaving Tittle in complete control. The Giants rolled to a 4-2 record in their first six games. And the Washington Redskins they were meeting had an even better record. The Redskins, behind the passing combination of quarterback Norm Snead and flanker Bobby Mitchell, had also won four of six. But unlike the Giants, they did not have two losses. Instead, they had tied twice.

Because he was nearly 3,000 miles from his home in Atherton, California, Tittle stayed at a hotel during the football season. Instead of getting out of bed as soon as he woke up, Tittle would lie there for a while, staring at the ceiling. On the morning of the Washington game, he went over the plays he would use and thought about the different defenses the Redskins might throw at him.

Then he reached over to the night table, grabbed the blue Giant playbook and went over the plays again, just to make sure he had them right. When he was finally satisfied, he got up, dressed, and went downstairs.

At breakfast he went over a few more plays with Coach Sherman and then got ready to leave for the stadium. He boarded the bus at 11:15 A.M.

The bus trip through the nearly empty streets of Manhattan was quiet and uneventful. Soon Tittle was in the locker room, slipping on a gray sweatshirt to protect himself against the late October cold of New York.

As he stepped onto the field for pre-game drills, the fans greeted Y.A. warmly. But the greeting was small compared to the one he received the second time he walked out. This time he was in his full uniform with the familiar "14" sewn on the front and back of his jersey.

Finally, the big stadium clock reached 2:00 P.M. —game time. Now Y.A. Tittle's workday really began.

Through most of the first quarter the game was a tight defensive duel. Then, with five minutes remaining in the quarter, Snead and Mitchell combined on a 44-yard scoring play for the Redskins.

Tittle, staying with his game plan of first establishing the running attack, then going to the air, brought the Giants back down the field after the Redskin kickoff. Combining the running of fullback Alex Webster with the pass-catching of tight end Joe Walton, split end Del Shofner and flanker Frank

Gifford, Tittle moved New York swiftly to the Washington 22-yard line.

Then Joe Morrison came into the game as a replacement for Gifford. "I brought a play in," said Morrison. "It was supposed to be a pass to Del. But I was all alone and Y.A. saw me, so he threw it to me." Morrison caught the ball and scored. Tittle's ability to see and hit the open man was one of his strong points. While he would always try to perform the play just as it had been drawn on the blackboard or in the playbook, he could also act on his own, if the occasion warranted it.

The Giants were now even, 7-7. In the second period, the big Giant defense rose up and began stopping the Washington attack as cornerback Erich Barnes shut off Mitchell. The first time the Giants had the ball in the second quarter Tittle moved them down to the Washington 5-yard line. Then, calling a rollout, he spotted Walton standing all alone in the end zone and drilled the ball into Joe's stomach. As a result, New York had a 14-7 lead.

The Redskins refused to give up and came back to score on a 24-yarder to Fred Dugan. But again Tittle brought his team back down the field on a time-eating drive. Finally, with the ball on the 1-yard line and third down, he faked Webster into the line, stepped back and flipped a short pass to Morrison for a 21-13 lead. And that's the way the first half ended.

Y.A., or "Yat," as he was also known, had put in

Good pass protection helps Tittle against the Redskins.

nearly a full day's work in the first half alone. He completed eleven of fifteen passes for over 200 yards and three touchdowns.

The Giants went into their locker room and relaxed—all except Tittle. Too keyed up to rest, he walked around the room, urging his teammates on. "Yat has the enthusiasm of a high school kid," said Gifford. "This is great for our young players. When they see a 36-year-old man get so fired up, they have to get excited, too. Heck, so do I, and I'm no kid."

Tittle fired the team up all right but, as soon as the second half began, Washington quickly took some of the spirit out of them. On the first play from scrimmage, Mitchell ran straight down-field, took a long pass from Snead on the Giant 45 and sailed right on into the N.Y. end zone to complete an 80-yard scoring play. The Giant lead was now down to one point, 21-20.

Now was the time Tittle needed the big play. Unless he rallied his Giants, the whole pattern of the game might be turned in the Redskins' favor. The only way to do it, he thought, was to fill the air with passes. And he did just that. First to Shofner. Then to Gifford. Back to Shofner. A quickie to Walton. After four passes, the Giants were on the Washington 32.

Now was the time to go for the touchdown. Tittle and Shofner decided to try a fake square-out and then go long. "I had studied the films," said Shofner, "and I saw that defensive halfback Claude Crabb was most vulnerable on a square-out pattern. We figured he'd be expecting a square-out again and we went long." Shofner burst off the line, ran ten steps, faked to his left and cut behind Crabb. Tittle timed the throw perfectly and laid it right in Del's hands for his fourth touchdown pass of the day.

Just as the Redskins had deflated the Giant spirit by their long scoring pass a few minutes earlier, Tittle had managed to undermine the overly confident Washington team by his passing attack.

When the Giants got the ball again, Tittle continued his assault. Moving New York back down the field, he threw a 26-yard touchdown strike to Walton for a 35-20 lead. Then the Giants rose up again and stopped the Skins, forcing them to punt to New York on the Giants' 23.

The Giants moved to a first down. Two running plays failed to gain and on third down, Tittle went back to pass. The Redskins sent two linebackers on a blitz. Tittle scampered back, his ankle-high cleats hopping around to avoid the Washington rushers in their white jerseys. He ducked under a swinging forearm, then moved up two steps when he saw his pocket crumbling around him. Out of the corner of his eye he spotted Gifford streaking down the right sideline. He whipped the ball in that sidearm style of his, floating it some 50 yards downfield. Gifford picked it off on the 20 and raced in for the touchdown. It was a 63-yard scoring pass—the sixth one of the day for Tittle.

The NFL record for touchdown passes in one game was seven, set by the Chicago Bears' Sid Luckman in 1943 and tied by the Philadelphia Eagles' Adrian Burk in 1954. But Tittle wasn't thinking about records. "The most important thing is winning," he said. He knew the Giants had to win the game if they wanted to make sure that Washington didn't run away with the Eastern title.

Still, Tittle couldn't help but be aware of the record he was approaching. After his sixth touchdown pass, he walked over to Kyle Rote, one of the Giant coaches, and said: "Some of the fellows want

Tittle hands off to fullback Alex Webster late in the Redskin game. But when rushes didn't gain ground, Y.A. passed—for a seventh touchdown.

me to go for the record." Rote told him: "Keep using the same plays and if they work for another touchdown, fine."

And that's just what he did. He used the same plays he had been studying all week, the same plays he had gone over in his hotel room that morning. They worked and the Giants soon found themselves back down on the Redskins' 6-yard line. From there Tittle sent Webster into the line twice, but the big fullback couldn't make a yard.

Y.A. called for a quick slant-in pass to Walton. At the snap of the ball he scurried back, set up, and threw over the outstretched arms of the straining Washington linemen. The ball thudded into Walton's midsection. Touchdown!

Tittle had now matched the existing record, and with eight minutes left, he still had plenty of time to break it. But the next time the Giants got the ball Tittle called three running plays and a punt. And the time after that, he called the same sequence. And still a third time, he called the same thing.

Finally, the gun sounded and the aging quarterback shyly trotted off the field with his head down, seemingly unaware of the tremendous ovation the fans were giving him. The Giants were 49-34 winners. But the biggest winner of all was Y.A. Tittle. He had completed his day's work with twenty-seven completions in thirty-nine attempts for 505 yards, and seven touchdowns—one of the most remarkable passing performances in NFL history. And it could have been even greater if Y.A. had gone to the air the last three times the Giants had the ball.

Why didn't he? "It wouldn't have been in good taste," he said in the locker room later. "It would have looked like too much individualism."

Despite Tittle's humility, the greatness of his performance didn't pass unnoticed by his teammates. They knew all about records and they knew all about great passing shows. Frank Gifford, who had been around for eleven pro seasons, summed up the players' feelings. After the reporters had left the locker room, he walked over to Y.A. and said: "Yat, that was the greatest passing performance I've ever seen."

8 / All-Star Surprise

CHICAGO: August 2, 1963—When Ron VanderKelen was growing up in Green Bay, Wisconsin, he dreamed of one day playing with the mighty Green Bay Packers. Instead, as leader of the 1963 College All-Stars, he found himself playing *against* them.

The most amazing thing of all, however, was that VanderKelen was on the field with the professionals. Less than a year before he had been an obscure substitute quarterback at the University of Wisconsin. His college playing time added up to exactly ninety seconds.

After an outstanding career at Preble High in Green Bay, Ron had enrolled at Wisconsin in 1958. The following year he was the third-string quarterback for the varsity and played in only one game. The next season, just when he thought he had a good chance to win the starting job, he hurt his knee. The resulting operation forced him to miss the entire season.

In 1961 he had recovered from the knee operation but ran into another kind of problem. Ron had trouble with his grades, was declared ineligible for football and dropped out of school. "When I left school," he said, "I worked for a construction company but I always read about Wisconsin. There was no doubt about what I wanted to do—return to school, become eligible, and play Wisconsin football."

VanderKelen came back to school in January, 1962, and was finally ready to play in the fall. He earned the starting job in the fourth game of the year, after he came off the bench to lead the Badgers to a 42-14 victory over Iowa.

Even though Ron paced Wisconsin to an 8-1 record and the Big Ten championship, the pro scouts hadn't given him a second look. None of the National Football League teams, in fact, even considered him good enough to draft. As a quarterback, Ron was a scrambler. He didn't like to stay in the relative safety of the pocket formed by his offensive linemen. Instead he would run around behind the line of scrimmage, dodging tacklers and looking for the open man. The NFL scouts figured that nobody with this kind of style could make it in the pros.

But Ron changed everyone's minds with a single game. His performance in the 1962 Rose Bowl, played on New Year's Day, turned him from a pro reject into a national hero. Ron put on the greatest individual performance in the history of the Rose Bowl. He completed 33 of 48 passes for 401 yards and two touchdowns. He scored another touchdown himself on a run. Although the unbeaten Trojans of the University of Southern California managed to hang on for a wild 42-37 victory, VanderKelen was the talk of America the next day. And suddenly the pro teams changed their opinions about Ron VanderKelen.

Because no NFL team had drafted him, Ron was a free agent. He didn't belong to anybody, and any team that wanted him had to get in line and make an offer. After considering all the offers, Ron signed with the Minnesota Vikings.

On the night of his game with the All-Stars, however, VanderKelen needed more than memories of last January's Rose Bowl heroics. For this was no ordinary team the College All-Stars were facing. These were the Green Bay Packers, the World Champions of professional football. It's no wonder that none of the experts and few of the 65,000 fans in Soldier Field gave the College All-Stars a chance.

On paper the Packers seemed invincible. In winning the 1962 NFL title, they had lost only a single game. They had Bart Starr, the league's leading quarterback, the man who had beaten the All-Stars only a year earlier by throwing five touchdown passes. And they had Jim Taylor, a fullback who seemed to prefer running over defenders to running around them. Protecting Starr and opening holes for Taylor was the Packers' awesome offensive line,

The Packer lineup sounded like the NFL All-Star team: (from left to right) Fuzzy Thurston, Jim Ringo, Jerry Kramer, Forrest Gregg, Ron Kramer.

unanimously acclaimed as the best in football.

Tough as the Packers seemed on offense, their defense was even stronger. In fourteen regular-season games the previous year, they had given up only 143 points, an average of barely ten a game. The All-Stars would have to run against men like Willie Davis, the Packers' monstrous defensive end, and

Henry Jordan, equally immovable at tackle. If the All-Stars chose to throw, they would have to contend with defensive backs like Herb Adderley and Willie Wood. To call the present game an overmatch was being charitable to the underdog collegians. A probable slaughter seemed closer to the truth.

At the time of the first annual game between the best of the college players and the NFL champions in 1934, the two teams had been evenly matched. At that time pro football was not nearly as popular as it is today. In addition, some of the best college players never turned professional. So in the early years the College All-Stars were able to make respectable showings. In fact, in the first five games the NFL champions won only once, while the All-Stars won twice. The other two games ended in ties.

As the years rolled along, however, the pros began to assert their superiority. Their players were drawn from the most outstanding of each year's college stars. And the year's championship NFL team was the best team in the league. Most important, the pros had played together as a team throughout the entire season.

The All-Stars, by comparison, met for the first time only a couple of weeks before the game. In the short time available, the All-Stars had to be shaped into a team. And they had to become not just an ordinary team, but a team capable of beating the world champions.

All-Star halfback Charley Mitchell (21) of the University

of Washington runs a sweep against the Packers.

Still the powerful Packers scored the first touchdown, and they did it so easily that the experts thought they would run the All-Stars off the field. After recovering a fumble, the Packers drove right through the heart of the All-Star defense. When Taylor slashed over from the 2-yard line, the All-Stars looked as if they were in for a long night. Jerry Kramer kicked the extra point and the NFL champions had a 7-0 lead.

The All-Stars came right back, though, on a long drive and seemed headed for a touchdown of their own. But their drive stalled on the Packer 13, and they had to settle for a 20-yard field goal by Bob Jencks of Miami University in Ohio.

Then, to the surprise of virtually everyone in Soldier Field, the All-Stars actually took the lead. Tom Janik, a defensive back from little Texas A&I, intercepted a pass and returned it 28 yards. Iowa's Larry Ferguson ran the ball in from the 6, Jencks kicked the extra point and, incredibly, the All-Stars were ahead, 10-7. But Kramer evened the score with a field goal for the pros, so the two teams entered the final quarter with the score 10-10.

The All-Stars had done the unexpected. They had put up a good fight for three quarters. But at this point everyone expected the championship superiority of the Packers to show. Taylor had been having his troubles running against the All-Stars' defensive line. The All-Stars' front four—Fred Miller of Louisiana State, Bobby Bell of Minnesota,

Lee Roy Jordan of Alabama, and Texas A&M's Lee Roy Caffey—had held the great Packer fullback in check after his early touchdown. But could they keep it up? Or would the pressure and their own lack of experience against the pros finally get to them?

As if in answer, the All-Stars forged back into the lead early in the fourth quarter on another field goal by Jencks, this time from 33 yards out. With a little more than three minutes left, the All-Stars found themselves with a third down and 4 yards to go on their own 27. If they failed to get the first down, they would have to punt and give the Packers a chance to win.

This was the time for VanderKelen the scrambler, VanderKelen the gambler. He rolled to his right, dodged a tackler, and threw a little pass to Pat Richter, an All-America end and his former teammate at Wisconsin. Richter caught the ball, got away from Jess Whittenton, the Green Bay cornerback, and suddenly found himself in the clear. The result was a 74-yard touchdown, with another extra point contributed by Jencks. The All-Stars had a 20-10 lead with less than three minutes to play.

The game was nearly over when the Packers got the final score on a 1-yard plunge by Taylor. But it made no difference. When the gun went off moments later, the All-Stars had achieved the seemingly impossible. They had beaten the World Champion Green Bay Packers, 20-17.

Late-blossoming Ron VanderKelen tells an announcer about the upset while All-Star Coach Otto Graham looks on.

And the one most responsible was Ron Vander-Kelen, the young man whom nobody had wanted a few months earlier. He completed nine of eleven passes for 141 yards and he made the big play when it counted. Most amazing of all, he had outplayed Bart Starr, the finest quarterback in the NFL.

After VanderKelen's brilliant performance in the Rose Bowl, one sportswriter had written: "Grid-iron historians may well mark this game as the day when the rah-rah boys caught up with the pros. The scramble and pass patterns of VanderKelen and

Company could be the wave of the immediate future in pro football."

Not one of the 65,000 people who saw the game in person, or the millions more who watched it on television, would have been inclined to argue the point.

9/Nevers'
One Man Show

CHICAGO: November 28, 1929—Thanksgiving was just another game day for Ernie Nevers, the player-coach of the Chicago Cardinal football team. He went into the kitchen of his Oak Street apartment and broiled a steak for breakfast. There might be a traditional turkey dinner later. But at the moment the 6-foot 1-inch, 210-pound fullback was really more interested in bear—Chicago Bear.

This was the day Ernie and the rest of the Cardinals would battle the Bears for the championship of Chicago. Since neither team seemed to be getting anywhere in the National Football League race, the important contest was the one that would prove who was the top dog in Chicago. A game earlier in the season had ended in a scoreless tie, which settled nothing.

Nevers, experienced far beyond his 26 years, had proved himself to be a remarkable athlete. He was not only a top performer on a football field but he had also been a major-league baseball player and had even had a fling at professional basketball.

Born in Willow River, Minnesota, in 1903, Ernie had started out as a tackling dummy at Superior Central High School in Superior, Wisconsin. "I was live bait in the tackling drills," he said. "I would stand in the sawdust pit and let the other kids tackle and block me. I wasn't allowed to move around. The only difference between me and a regular tackling dummy was that I could talk and I didn't have a rope around my neck."

By the time the Nevers family moved to Santa Rosa, California, Ernie had become a star fullback. He led the Santa Rosa High team to an all-winning season. (Back at Superior Central he had already led the basketball team to a state championship.)

The powerful, blond-haired Nevers first gained national acclaim as a football player at Stanford University in Palo Alto, California. At the start of his senior year, however, Ernie broke an ankle in scrimmage. He was sidelined for most of the season, and when he finally got back into action he broke the other ankle. This would have been sufficient to end the collegiate playing career of the average senior athlete, but Ernie was not average. He was already being acknowledged as an "Iron Man."

The Stanford Indians, as it happened, were selected for the Rose Bowl game, where they would meet Knute Rockne's legendary Notre Dame team with its Four Horsemen. The cast was taken off

Nevers' ankle only a week before the game. But immediately Nevers told his coach, Glenn "Pop" Warner, that he was ready to play. And he was. Nevers played sixty minutes and had a magnificent day.

"He tore our line to shreds, he ran the ends, forward-passed and kicked," Rockne said. "True, once we held him on four downs on the 1-yard line, but by that time Nevers was exhausted, and I had sent in two fresh guards and a fresh tackle to stop this fury in football boots."

Nevers visits with Pop Warner, his college coach. Warner, who also coached Jim Thorpe, rated Nevers the better of the two.

Even so, the blond bull wasn't able to swing the game. Notre Dame won the Rose Bowl, 27-10.

The next season, 1925, Nevers received $25,000 to play a number of exhibition games against a team headed by another football immortal, Red Grange. Subsequently he joined the Duluth Eskimos of the NFL. In one year the Eskimos played twenty-nine games, including five in eight days, and Iron Man Nevers sat out only a total of twenty-seven minutes during the entire season.

Nor was he content to limit himself to football. In baseball Nevers was so highly regarded as a right-handed pitcher that he played for the St. Louis Browns, starting in 1926. He remained active in the majors for three years. And during that time he played a role, though unwillingly, in Babe Ruth's record home-run campaign of 1927. Ernie gave up two home runs (numbers eight and forty-one) as the Babe slammed his way to sixty.

Then Nevers suffered an injury which forced him back to the San Francisco Missions in the Pacific Coast League and cut short his baseball career. He was still a vital, productive football player, however.

In the contest between the two Chicago pro teams on Thanksgiving Day, Ernie was the star of the team, in addition to being Cardinal coach. As was his custom, after finishing his pre-game steak, he took a taxi to Comiskey Park, the Cardinals' home field. In the clubhouse he was joined by such bulwarks of the team as tackles Duke Slater and Walt Kiesling and backs Gene Rose, Cobb Rooney and Mickey McDonald. As player-coach, Nevers was paid $10,000 for the season. The others received as little as $100 a game.

Despite their low scale of pay by today's standards, all were professionals, and they especially wanted to win this game. Usually the Bears took the city championship, but today Nevers had calmly but firmly announced to his team in the locker room:

"This one is for us."

The day was cold, the field was icy, and there were fewer than 8,000 shivering spectators in the bleachers when the game started. A third of the way through the first quarter, Nevers, with help from a powerful line, went 10 yards inside tackle for a touchdown. His kick was wide, but before the quarter ended he had added another touchdown, this time on a 5-yard plunge over center. Nevers' place-kick was good, giving the Cardinals a 13-0 advantage.

Because of the icy surface of the frozen field, Nevers had decided that the game would have to be won on the line. The Cardinals, who used the double wing formation, would not run to the outside. They would not attempt much passing, either.

Fullback Nevers coached, called the plays, ran the ball, punted, and place-kicked. In the second

Nevers, with ball, tumbles to the ground after a gain.

quarter he scored another touchdown, 6 yards over the middle, and his place-kick made it 20-0 at half-time.

The Bears were getting nowhere. Unable to make any headway on the ground with their star Red Grange, they went to the air in the third period. Walt Holmer connected on several passes, one of which was a 60-yard scoring play to Garland Grange, Red's brother. Holmer's place-kick failed, and the Cardinals stood confident at 20-6. Then Nevers blasted across from the 1-yard line and added the placement, raising the score to 27-6.

The crowd began chanting, "Give the ball to Nevers." One didn't have to be good in arithmetic to know that Ernie had scored all twenty-seven Cardinal points. He had been carrying the ball on an average of three out of every four chances. And he would continue at this pace.

In the first ten minutes of the fourth period, Nevers scored twice more—on a short plunge and on a 10-yard rush. His first try for the extra point failed because of a bad pass from center, but Ernie made the next one. Nobody had ever scored so many points in an NFL game.

It would have been quite accurate to quote the score as: Nevers 40, Bears 6. And that's how the game ended.

10/Marathon Football

GREEN BAY: December 26, 1965—Bart Starr took the ball from center Ken Bowman at his 15-yard line and dropped back to pass. On the first play of the game, Green Bay was wasting no time in testing Baltimore's pass defense.

Starr spotted tight end Bill Anderson cutting toward the left sideline and threw. Anderson caught the pass, but before he could tuck it into his body he was hit by scrambling cornerback Lenny Lyles. The ball popped out of Anderson's hands, and Don Shinnick, a Colt linebacker, scooped it up at the Packer 25 and started down the sideline.

As Shinnick neared the goal line, Starr angled over to try and prevent the game's first touchdown. Shinnick had two blockers in front of him, and the quarterback wanted to break up the interference so another Packer could grab the linebacker. But safetyman Jim Welch knocked Starr down, and Shinnick scampered into the end zone untouched, the ball held high above his head as a gesture of triumph.

Tom Matte, a Colt halfback, was an unlikely hero at quarterback.

For the Colts, there was reason to be joyous. For the Packers, there were reasons to be sad. Not only had the Colts rushed off to a 7-0 lead, but the brave Starr had been knocked to the ground, holding his ribs in pain. Just thirty-one seconds had ticked off in the game, and already the Packers were without their key offensive weapon.

Baltimore had an unexpected break in its favor. But the Colts were due. During the course of the 1965 season, they had lost their two top quarterbacks—the incomparable Johnny Unitas, with a knee injury, and his competent back-up man, Gary Cuozzo, with a shoulder separation. That left Coach Don Shula with no true quarterback. All he had was a halfback, Tom Matte, who had played quarterback in college. And at Ohio State, Matte was more of a running quarterback than a passer. Matte had made his debut as a Colt quarterback only a week before the showdown with the Packers and the result was astounding: he led Baltimore to a 20-17 victory over the Los Angeles Rams. The upset victory threw the NFL Western Division standings into a tie between Baltimore and Green Bay.

Now, thirty-one seconds of playing time after the Colts' Lou Michaels had kicked off to start the game at Green Bay's Lambeau Field, the left-footed booter kicked off again. The Packers' Herb Adderley took the kick at the 1-yard line and worked his way out to the 18.

As the Packer offensive unit trotted onto the field, Starr remained seated on the bench, trying to soothe his injured ribs. In his place came veteran Zeke Bratkowski, one of the better reserve signal callers in the league. Taking no chances on a repeat of the first play of the game, Bratkowski handed to Paul Hornung, and the celebrated halfback dashed for 7 yards to the 25.

Bratkowski then went to Jim Taylor, the other half of the potent Packer running duo, who got 2 yards. On third down, Taylor banged off tackle for 3 yards and a first down.

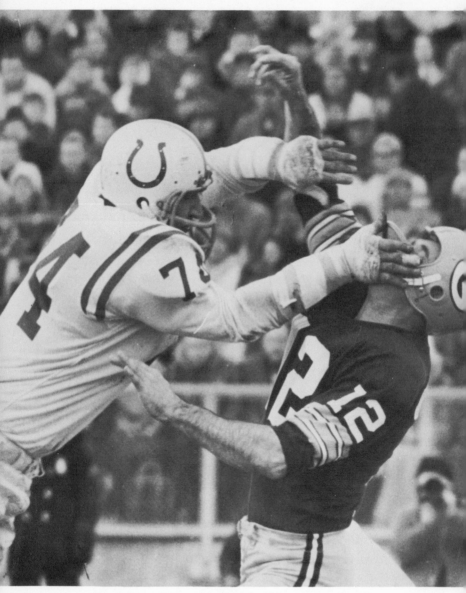

The Colts' Billy Ray Smith (74) tries to break quarter-back Zeke Bratkowski's pass.

Now Bratkowski tried his first pass, firing to Anderson, who held onto the ball this time for an 8-yard gain. Back to the ground, with Hornung racing around left end for 7 yards. Hornung carried the ball again, plowing 5 yards. But he fumbled when he was hit, and cornerback Lyles, who had forced the fumble from Anderson, fell on the ball at the 50.

The Colts finally had the ball on offense, and Matte came onto the field for the final test in the cram course he had taken the previous week. But this time, Matte was allowed to bring a "cheat sheet" with him—a card with some of the Colt plays taped to his left wrist so he would not forget them.

Matte didn't have to look at the card for the first play. He called a simple handoff to halfback Lenny Moore, and Moore banged into the line. That was as far as he got and it was also as far as Matte got, because Moore lost the ball and Packer safety Tom Brown fell on it.

Although Starr was on the sidelines, trying to throw a ball, Bratkowski was still the quarterback when the Packer offensive unit returned to the field. This time they hoped to hold onto the ball. Hornung ran for 6, then 1, and Taylor just missed the first down with a 2-yard gain to the Baltimore 41. Instead of trying for the first down, though, Coach Vince Lombardi sent in Don Chandler for a field goal try from the 47.

Colt halfback Lenny Moore (24) high-steps

around the Packer line.

The kick was short, however, so the Colts still led, 7-0, after almost seven minutes of play. During this seven minutes there had been three fumbles, one touchdown, one unsuccessful field-goal attempt and one injured quarterback. The remaining time in the first quarter was dominated by Chandler and Tom Gilburg, Chandler punting twice and Gilburg three times.

The second quarter started the same way—with Chandler getting off his third punt. But then Matte started generating the first Colt offensive drive. With Matte running twice and passing once to Moore, and with Jerry Hill running seven times, the Colts marched to the Green Bay 8-yard line. But on third down, with 3 yards to go for the crucial first down, Tony Lorick was stopped, and Baltimore had to settle for a 15-yard field goal by Michaels with 5:29 left in the first half.

Now it was the Packers' turn to threaten. Bratkowski's 12-yard pass to Carroll Dale, an 8-yarder to Hornung and a pass interference call against safety Jerry Logan, a 47-yard penalty, moved the ball to the Baltimore 9. Bratkowski hit Anderson for an 8-yard gain to the 1, but there the Colt line toughened, stopping Taylor and Hornung for no gains.

Forsaking a certain field goal, Bratkowski tried Taylor again on fourth down, but the fullback was hit by linebacker Dennis Gaubatz and fumbled. Taylor fell on the ball, inches short of the goal line, The half ended with the Colts leading, 10-0.

Baltimore got the ball at the start of the third quarter but couldn't go anywhere with it. And when Gilburg went back to punt, the snap from center nearly sailed over his head. Gilburg pulled the ball down and ran with it, getting back to Baltimore's 35 before he was caught.

The Packers wasted no time in taking advantage of the break. After Taylor ran for a yard, Bratkowki connected with Dale on a 33-yard pass to the 1-yard line. Hornung smashed across behind a Jerry Kramer block on the next play for Green Bay's first points.

Trailing by only three points, Green Bay threatened once more in the quarter, but Bobby Boyd intercepted a Bratkowski pass at the Baltimore 19. Logan stopped another Packer drive the same way after three minutes had elapsed in the fourth quarter, picking off a Bratkowski toss at the Colt 8.

By now, both Bratkowski and Coach Lombardi had become a little disturbed at the bad fortune the quarterback was having with his passes. But Lombardi had to stay with his 33-year-old reserve quarterback because there was no way Starr could do anything but hold the ball for place-kicks.

As far as Bratkowski was concerned, he wasn't going to let a couple of interceptions affect his style of play. The next time the Packers got the ball, after Gilburg's sixth punt, Bratkowski tossed to Boyd Dowler, then to Hornung, moving the ball to the Green Bay 48.

A personal foul call against Colt tackle Billy Ray Smith took the ball into Baltimore territory at the 43. The Packers had less than seven minutes to come from behind.

Bratkowski, mixing his plays effectively, led the Packers all the way to the Colt 15. Suddenly it was third down and a crucial moment for both teams. The Colts got set for a pass—which turned out to be a good guess. But instead of throwing to Bill Anderson or Boyd Dowler or Carroll Dale, Bratkowski went to fullback Taylor. And the pass misfired. The Colts held onto their 10-7 lead.

Lombardi decided to tie the score first, then worry about a victory. In came Starr and Chandler —Starr to hold, Chandler to kick. Starr called the signals, rookie Bill Curry snapped the ball, Starr smoothly put it down at the 22 and Chandler stepped up to kick. The ball sailed toward the goal posts, and field judge James Tunney raised his hands, signaling that the game was tied, 10-10, with only one minute and fifty-eight seconds to go.

Immediately Michaels, the Colt kicker and defensive left end, rushed to referee Norm Schachter and protested that the kick had gone wide to the left. Several other Colts joined in. But Schachter merely told them the official in the end zone had called the kick good.

The three points stood, of course, and the Colts had one last chance to secure the victory which they already thought had been theirs. Matte threw an incomplete pass, Moore ran for 5 yards and Matte for 1. That brought in Gilburg for another punt. With 27 seconds left, the Packers had their last chance.

Bratkowski lost 4 yards with a pass to halfback Tom Moore, but hit Taylor for 20 yards to the Baltimore 46. The Packer kicking team rushed onto the field for a last-second Chandler field goal try, but the gun went off, signaling the end of regulation time.

Thus, for the second time in history, an NFL game was to be decided by a "sudden-death" overtime. The first had come in 1958 when the same Colts defeated the New York Giants, 23-17, for the league championship after eight minutes and fifteen seconds of extra play.

The Packers got first chance at the winning points as Moore took Michaels' kickoff at the 2 and raced to the 22. Taylor smashed for 2 yards on first down, but on the next two downs Bratkowski missed on passes to Dale and Anderson. Chandler came in again, this time to punt.

The Colts had no better luck. Gilburg punted for the eighth time. Less than two minutes later Chandler punted for the fifth time. When the Colts got the ball back, Matte found some gaping holes in the Packer line. He darted through for 9 yards on first down, 5 on second and 8 more on first. He had moved the ball to the Green Bay 37.

The Colts needed just 2 yards to keep the drive going, but the Packers bottled up Moore for a loss and then knocked Matte down behind the line. Although it was the end of the Colts' drive, it was not the end of their chance to win their second sudden-death game. As Michaels and the rest of the Baltimore place-kicking unit trotted onto the field, everyone on the sidelines and in the crowd was tense.

The teams on the field got set. Bobby Boyd, the Colts' holder, got down at the Green Bay 47, his right knee on the ground, his left leg outstretched. Michaels stepped back, swung his left leg and checked the angle. Suddenly, everything went wrong. The snap from center hit in front of Boyd, and the six-year veteran had to reach out and scoop up the ball. He hurriedly placed it down, but Michaels' timing had already been thrown off, and his kick fell short of the winning field goal.

So with eight minutes gone in the extra period, the Packers were 80 yards away from a score.

Elijah Pitts replaced Hornung, who had twisted a knee, and he ran for 4 yards. Bratkowski then turned to his favorite target, Anderson, and hit him as he crossed toward the center of the field and hooked into an open spot. The play went for 18 yards and gave the Packers a first down at their 42.

Bratkowski went back to the ground as Pitts dashed for 6 yards and Taylor for 5 and another first down. Taylor bolted for 3 more yards. Then Bratkowski spotted Dale breaking between two defenders and fired to him for an 18-yard gain to the 26.

Don Chandler's field goal, with Starr (15) holding, finally ends the NFL's longest game.

Back to the ground again, but the Colts stopped Taylor for no gain. Pitts, however, smashed for 4 yards, and Green Bay was down to the 22. Bratkowski, of course, had no intention of taking any chances with a possible pass interception now that he was in field goal range. He handed to Taylor, who burst for 4 more yards to the 18.

Now it was the Packers' turn to try a field goal. They were in much better position than the Colts had been five minutes earlier.

Starr, his ribs still aching, shuffled out from the sidelines. Chandler trotted next to him. Starr called the obvious signals in the huddle and the Packers broke for their positions. Starr walked to the 25 and got down on his left knee. He could feel the soreness in his ribs, but his concentration was focused on the ball which Curry held at the line.

Chandler stood a few feet behind Starr, slightly hunched over, his arms dangling at his sides. He had been a New York Giant in the overtime title game in 1958—but he hadn't been a place-kicker then. He was now, though, and it was he who could end the game.

Curry snapped the ball back to Starr, Starr swiftly placed it down at the 25 and Chandler stepped and kicked. All eyes followed the end-over-end flight of the ball. It sailed cleanly between the uprights, leaving no room for protest.

The longest game in the National League's history was over, after thirteen minutes and thirty-nine seconds of extra play. And the Green Bay Packers had beaten the Baltimore Colts, 13-10, for the 1965 Western Conference championship.

11/100 Yards Plus

PHILADELPHIA: November 15, 1953—Buddy Young of the Baltimore Colts stepped back to his own goal line and stared into the sky. The day was overcast so there was no sun to make him squint. It would be easy to see the football against the gray clouds. As he watched Bobby Walston of the Philadelphia Eagles teeing up the ball for the opening kickoff, his heart began to race with excitement.

He always felt this way at the start of every game —excited, but never nervous or tense. He hoped the ball would be kicked to him, for he wanted to run it back as far as he could to give his team an opening advantage. This was characteristic of Buddy Young, the former Illinois All-America now in his seventh year as a professional player. He had won national acclaim in two varsity seasons at Illinois during an era when few Negroes played football for big-name colleges. In those days, a Negro had to be exceptional to gain acceptance on a team. And Buddy Young *was* exceptional, both as a person and as an athlete.

As a boy, Claude Young had grown up in a poor section of Chicago. There were nine children in the Young family, and Claude's parents separated when he was eight. Although Claude was small, he was an excellent athlete. He ran with the speed of a sprinter and played a good deal of sandlot football. When his local high school coach told Buddy he was too small to play for his team, the boy found a coach at another school in a different district who was willing to give him a tryout. As soon as the coach told Buddy he could make the team, Buddy moved in with an aunt who lived in that school district. The name of the school was Wendell Phillips.

Buddy not only made the team as a running back, he became a star. In 1943, he scored twenty-five touchdowns in ten games to help Wendell Phillips clinch the public-school title. He also starred on the track team. A whole new world was opening before him. "From the very first," he said, "my teammates showed a very friendly feeling. I knew I had my first chance, and if I worked hard, maybe I could get what I wanted out of life."

By the time he was ready for college, Buddy had scholarship offers from Michigan, Marquette, Oregon, Drake and Illinois. He chose Illinois, where he went out for football and track. Buddy's idol was Jesse Owens, the great Ohio State track star who had won four gold medals at the 1936 Olympic Games in Berlin. Owens tried to persuade Buddy to abandon football and concentrate on track, but

At Illinois, Buddy Young earned a bundle of track medals and at the same time developed speed for football.

Buddy liked football too much to give it up. He didn't neglect his work on the cinder paths, however. In the Big Ten track meet in 1944, he won the 100-yard dash, the 220 and the broad jump, and very nearly won the low hurdles. Had he done so, he would have duplicated a feat accomplished by Owens nine years earlier.

In his sophomore year at Illinois, Buddy ran for thirteen touchdowns to tie Red Grange's one-season record in the Big Ten. One of his runs was a 74-yard sweep against Notre Dame. The United States was still fighting in World War II so the following season Buddy was in training with the Merchant Marine. He was recruited by the football team at the base in Fleet City, California. In one game he ran for touchdowns of 94 and 88 yards against the El Toro Marines, giving Fleet City a 45-28 victory before 70,000 spectators in the Los Angeles Coliseum.

His coach at Fleet City, Bill Reinhard, said: "Buddy is the greatest player I ever saw. He will block and tackle with the best. He not only goes outside, but inside as well for me."

When he returned to Illinois in 1946, though, Buddy had his problems. He hurt his ankle early in the season and it never had a chance to heal properly. The breakaway runs became less frequent. The blazing speed with which he ran back kicks seemed to be missing. The sportswriters began to say that Buddy was through. He was back in fair shape for the final game of the regular-season campaign, however, and Illinois walloped Northwestern to win the Big Ten title. The Illini accepted an invitation to play in the Rose Bowl. Buddy later explained that, when the sportswriters wrote all the columns about his being through and voted him eighth as the Flop of the Year in the Associated Press poll, they gave him all the incentive he needed. He promised himself he would be ready for the Rose Bowl.

Actually he proved to be more than ready. He was nothing less than sensational at Pasadena. He tore loose for two touchdowns, and Illinois ripped favored UCLA, 45-14. Buddy Young was back on top again where he belonged. Then he caught everybody off balance by announcing that he would not return to Illinois for his senior year. He had married while in college, and now he had a young son, Claude, Jr. Buddy had to think about supporting a family, and he decided the way to do it was to play professional football.

Young signed to play with the New York Yankees of the new All-America Football Conference in 1947. For the next half-dozen years, Buddy dazzled football fans with his explosive running. At his height of 5 feet 5 inches and weight of 170 pounds, he was like a hard rubber ball that seemed to bounce up immediately after being pounded to the turf. His meteoric speed enabled him to run away from defenses, but he also had such perfect balance that he could feint defenders out of position.

After the AAFC merged with the National Football League in 1950, the Yankees went through a series of franchise shifts and in 1953 became the

Baltimore Colts. On the afternoon of the game between the Colts and the Eagles at Philadelphia, Buddy was in his seventh year as a pro. The Baltimore fans were so enthusiastic about their new football team that more than 5,000 of them had come by special trains and buses to see the game.

Buddy himself had gotten up about seven o'clock and gone to church services. At nine he boarded the team train for Philadelphia. His wife and son, and many of the other players' wives, followed on another section. When the train pulled into the North Philadelphia station at approximately 11:30 A.M., the players debarked and walked the few short blocks to Shibe Park.

Since there were still more than two hours until game time, the Colt players went out in their street clothes to inspect the field. Buddy felt the turf under his feet—it was dry and springy. "We've got a fast track today," he said to his roommate, Zollie Toth.

Some of the players drifted into the stands and sat down. Buddy joined them, taking a seat next to Art Donovan, the mammoth Colt defensive tackle. Donovan had found a concessionaire selling hot dogs and had ordered three of them. Spotting Buddy, he offered him a bite. "Here," he said, "they're good and hot." It was the only thing Buddy would eat all day.

Finally, the players went down to their dressing room and started to get ready for the game. Buddy began to feel his usual twinge of pre-game excitement. Over and over again, he kept visualizing what he would like to do with the ball if it came to him on the opening kickoff. He always silently rooted for his team to win the toss of the coin and have the option of receiving.

As he tugged on his jersey, he felt a sharp pain in his ribs. Several weeks earlier, Buddy had landed on the point of a football, then an opposing player had landed on top of him. Some cartilage in his rib cage had been torn loose. The injury wasn't serious enough to sideline him, but he had to wear heavy padding around it to protect himself from further injury.

In the pre-game warmup, Buddy ran plays at halfback with the first-string backfield, caught some passes and fielded kickoffs. He could feel the loose cartilage floating around inside him, but at least it was wrapped tightly, making him look a bit heavy in the chest. As the teams trotted off for their last-minute instructions, the captains met at midfield for the coin toss. The Colts won, and elected to receive.

Down in the Colt locker room, Coach Keith Molesworth spoke calmly and soberly to his players. He wasn't the type to deliver stirring pep talks. He just reminded the players of their individual assignments and let it go at that. Everyone knew by now what he had to do. Buddy sensed that the team was unusually keyed up, probably because so

Small but sure-footed, Young (76) easily out-maneuvers his opponents.

many Colt fans had come up from Baltimore.

When the teams eventually emerged on the field, the starting players were introduced individually. After his name was announced, Buddy huddled with the Colt starters in the middle of the field. "I'm going to take it up the middle," he told them. "Give me some blocking to the outside." Then he dropped back to his right safety position and waited. Now all he could do was hope the ball would come to him.

The whistle was blown, and Bobby Walston booted the ball. The kick wasn't especially high, but it was the kind Buddy liked. He could get a running start, even before the ball reached him; he also would have a clear view of how the enemy tacklers would be coming at him. He caught the ball on the run in his own end zone and headed up the right side of the field. He veered a little to the left and then back to the right again.

As he reached his own 35-yard line, Buddy saw a gaping hole in the middle of the Eagle defense. Only the Eagle safetyman was in front of him, and that player had come to a dead halt to see what Buddy would do next. Instantly Buddy turned on his blazing speed, running directly at the last Eagle defender, who remained stationary. Buddy knew he had him. He was moving, while the Eagle player was back on his heels waiting. As he got close to the safetyman, Buddy faked him out and then swung to his left. There was nothing but a clear field ahead. Buddy poured on the speed, his chunky legs pumping like pistons. He streaked across the goal line without anyone even touching him.

Buddy dropped the ball in the end zone, then turned and headed for the Baltimore bench. He was exhilarated by the run, of course; but he had no idea of the actual distance he had traveled. Other Colt players came up to him and pounded him on the back, congratulating him for the touchdown. But they, too, didn't realize he had just carried the opening kickoff 104 yards for a touchdown. It was the second-longest runback of a kickoff in NFL history!

After that, unfortunately, the game was all downhill for Buddy and the Colts. The Eagles scored on their first series of plays, tying the score. Then when Walston kicked off again, he deliberately kicked the ball along the ground. He wasn't taking any chances with another Buddy Young runback. But Buddy didn't do much else. His rib cage was sore and he couldn't run with any consistency. At halftime, the Eagles had built a 21-7 lead and Coach Molesworth told Buddy not to bother to go onto the field for the second half. The final score was Eagles 45, Colts 14.

By the time the bedraggled Colts returned to their locker room, Buddy was dressed and ready to leave for the train station. The dressing room was always too depressing after a defeat. On his way out, some sportswriters stopped him and told him about his runback. "One hundred and four yards, Buddy," one of them said. "Only Frank Seno of the Chicago Cardinals ever ran one back any longer." Buddy raised his eyebrows in surprise and managed to smile wanly. Despite their congratulations he couldn't forget the final figures on the scoreboard. Even a 104-yard touchdown couldn't change that unhappy story.

12/Electric Field

GREEN BAY: December 31, 1967—The thin sheet of ice was cracking under Bart Starr's cleats as he jogged from the sideline meeting with Coach Vince Lombardi to the Green Bay Packer huddle. With sixteen seconds left in the game, the Packers were trailing, 17-14. If they could somehow manage to pull ahead, they would become the only team ever to win three straight NFL championship games.

It was the coldest December 31st in Green Bay history. The 1967 National Football League championship game on Lambeau Field was supposed to be the first on an electrically heated field. But even the electricity couldn't overcome the thirteen-below-zero temperature.

"This field is still the warmest place in the state of Wisconsin," Lombardi said proudly.

Tom Landry, the Dallas Cowboy coach, was more concerned about the Packers than the weather. His team was looking for revenge. The previous year the Packers had beaten the Cowboys, 34-27, for the

Bart Starr's pass appears to "steam by" Cowboy defenders.

1966 NFL title. In that game, played at Dallas, the Cowboys had been driving for a possible tie and "sudden-death" overtime when an overanxious Cowboy lineman jumped offside near the Packer goal line. Two plays later the Packers' Tom Brown intercepted a Don Meredith pass to assure the victory.

"We'll be back," Cowboy quarterback Don Meredith had said at the time. And he was right.

During 1967 the Cowboys had ridden roughshod over their Eastern Conference opponents. Right from the beginning the Packers had a difficult time in the wild Western Conference.

Starr had had the worst game of his twelve-year pro football career on the opening day of the season. The Detroit Lions intercepted four of his passes in the first half, one more than he had suffered in all fourteen games of 1966. The Lions scored seventeen points in the half. But the Packers came back in the second half to salvage a tie.

There were four worse Sundays for Starr during the season. "Those were the four games I couldn't play," Starr said. A shoulder injury was followed by a rib injury, which was followed by a hand injury. In the process, Bart's opponents had intercepted his passes seventeen times prior to the NFL title rematch with the Cowboys.

With only sixteen seconds left in the championship game, Starr had yet to be intercepted. But he had been dropped on the frozen field eight times by Cowboy defenders. All in all, the lack of protection by the Green Bay linemen had resulted in Starr's being thrown for losses totaling 76 yards.

Obviously Bart was upset. But he remained silent —as silent as the Packers had come to expect him to be. He had arrived in Green Bay in 1956 as a quiet Seventeenth-round draft choice from the University of Alabama and had remained humble as he climbed the ladder of greatness.

But the setbacks he suffered in 1967 had shaken him. Even in an exhibition game with the Pittsburgh Steelers, he had surprised his teammates. Recovering from a smack in the mouth received after he released a pass, Starr verbally spanked the reserve lineman who had failed to hold his block.

"If I see that guy in here once more tonight," Starr said in the next huddle, "I'm not going to kick him in the can. I'm going to kick *you* in the can, right in front of all these people."

In the game against the Cowboys, however, Starr was not going to take the time to kick, either verbally or physically. He had thrown two touchdown passes to Boyd Dowler to give the Packers a 14-0 lead. The first was from the Cowboy 8-yard

Boyd Dowler (86), catching a touchdown pass against the Cowboys, always seemed to be in the right place at the right time.

line after the Packers had inched their way through
the stubborn Cowboy defensive line. The second
touchdown was a Bart Starr Special. With third
down and 1 yard to go on the Cowboy 43-yard line,
Bart gambled. Instead of having the fullback try
for the first down, Starr faded deep and threw the
touchdown pass to Dowler.

The 50,861 shivering football fanatics in their
Green Bay gold and green blankets, caps and muf-
flers were warming up for a big victory.

But not Willie Townes, Jethro Pugh, Bob Lilly
and George Andrie—the Cowboy front line. Later
in the second quarter defensive end Townes smacked
Starr and the ball went bouncing behind the quarterback. Andrie, the other end, picked up the football 7 yards from the goal line and was not touched
until he had stretched his 6-foot 7-inch frame into
the end zone.

Later Packer Willie Wood fumbled a punt on his
own 16-yard line. The Cowboys couldn't move the
ball but Danny Villaneuva kicked a 21-yard field
goal.

"We gave them ten easy points," Lombardi mut-
tered. "We gave them the momentum."

The Packers' 14-10 halftime lead stood until
Dallas scored on the first play of the fourth quarter.
The Cowboys ordered halfback Dan Reeves, a for-
mer college quarterback, to fake a run around end,
then throw the option pass. Reeves found flanker
Lance Rentzel all alone on the throw. Rentzel

Starr (15) dives for the crucial fourth-down score as

Mercein (30) signifies "touchdown."

caught the ball and dashed 50 yards downfield to score.

Ironically, Paul Hornung, the retired Packer "Golden Boy" who had made the option pass popular in the pros, was sitting on the Green Bay bench when Reeves made the play. Hornung was a guest of the Packers this day.

The score remained at 17-14 after an unsuccessful 40-yard Green Bay field-goal attempt by Don Chandler. The Cowboys then ran ten time-consuming plays, and Green Bay hopes dropped lower than the temperature.

When Starr led the Packer offensive unit onto the field with 4:50 left on the clock, the ball was 68 yards from the goal line and the Dallas defense was waiting to cut the Packers off at the pass.

Starr called a variety of plays: a pass to Donny Anderson for 6 yards, a run by Chuck Mercein for 7, a pass to Dowler for 9, a pass to Anderson again for 12.

Then Starr turned to Mercein, the former Yale fullback, who had been let go during the season by the New York Giants. Coach Lombardi had called him because he needed replacements for his injured fullbacks, Elijah Pitts and Jim Grabowski. "I almost ran to Green Bay after I hung up the phone," Mercein said. As it turned out, Lombardi got his money's worth.

Starr threw to Mercein, who galloped 19 yards to the Cowboy 11. With 1:11 left to play, Starr sent Mercein through the middle on a delay play and Chuck reached the 3-yard line. Fifty-four seconds to go and the Packers were still 3 yards short of the goal line, the victory and place in the pro football history books.

Starr sent Anderson into the line for a first down at the 1-yard line with thirty seconds left. After a quick huddle, Anderson tried again. No score. Starr called time out with twenty seconds left. Then he called the same play. The same result. Anderson slipped on the frozen ground.

With sixteen seconds left, Starr used the Packers' final time out. He went to the sideline to talk to Lombardi and assistant coach Phil Bengtson. Offensive tackle Forrest Gregg came over. They talked of the rock-solid ground and the decision that had to be made.

Then came Starr's gamble on third down. If the Packers didn't bring Chandler in to try a field goal, they would have to pass to score or stop the clock. A running play at this point would eat up the remaining time.

Gregg's breath preceded him as he trudged back to the huddle. An official was wiping off the ball and placing it a foot from the goal line when Starr jogged toward his command post in the Packer huddle.

As calm as if it were the opening play of an exhibition game, Starr called for a Mercein fake run up the middle. Starr added, "I'll keep the ball."

The Packers blocked for the fullback to run up the middle. And the Packers blocked for Bart Starr.

Starr dived between right guard Jerry Kramer and tackle Forrest Gregg. The first person to hit Starr was Mercein, who carried out his fake and lifted his hands like an official signaling a touchdown as he landed on Starr's back in the frozen end zone.

Starr had tears in his eyes as he got up. His touchdown had given the Packers their third straight NFL title. The final score, with Chandler's extra point, was 21-17.

13/Miracle Kicker

PITTSBURGH: September 24, 1967—Jim Bakken awoke at eight A.M. and looked out the window of his hotel room to check the weather. "All football players do that first," said Bakken, the 26-year-old place-kicker for the St. Louis Cardinals. "It's especially important to kickers. We don't want rain, but above all we don't want wind."

He had half his wish. The day was cloudy, but there was no real danger of rain. The wind, however, was whipping at 14 miles an hour from the northwest. Bakken sighed unhappily, for he knew that whatever kicks he would try against the Pittsburgh Steelers during the afternoon would have to buck that wind.

After getting dressed, the handsome, blond Bakken, whose 6-foot 2-inch, 200-pound frame looked curiously small when viewed against the tremendous bulk of most of his teammates, attended the Cardinal church service at eight-thirty. Then he went for his pre-game meal. At ten-fifteen, the forty

Bakken (25) clears the uprights for one of his record field goals against the Steelers.

St. Louis players broke up into smaller groups by positions for brief meetings. Bakken, a reserve flanker as well as the kicker, joined the receivers' group.

When the meeting was over, Bakken and a few other players chipped in for a cab to Pitt Stadium. Pro football players are as tense as caged animals on the day of a game. To these Cardinals, the short, early ride to the ballpark was a way of relieving the pre-game tension. "The team bus doesn't leave until eleven-thirty," said Bakken, "but I can't stand sitting around the hotel lobby with nothing to do. So some of us usually go to the park and get taped, then sit around and play solitaire or look at a program or just relax."

There was no reason for Bakken to be nervous. Since coming to the Cardinals in 1962, after the Los Angeles Rams had drafted him and turned him loose, Bakken had attempted 145 extra points. He had missed only one. In field-goal attempts, a more challenging art for the place-kicker, Bakken had been successful on 80 of 132 tries. Thus Bakken's confidence had been established early in his career at St. Louis. In fact, one day in 1964, he had commented that he "would like to break the NFL record of five field goals in a game." But Garo Yepremian, the Detroit Lions' soccer-style kicker from Cyprus, had beaten Bakken to that mark by kicking six in a single 1966 game. Now in Pittsburgh, less than one year after Yepremian's big performance,

Bakken felt only slightly envious of his Detroit counterpart.

The St. Louis team bus arrived, and soon the dressing room was filled with the massive bodies of the Cardinals as they donned their brilliant red-and-white uniforms. Then it was time to warm up, and Bakken suddenly realized that there was another reason why the day did not look promising for him. In addition to the problems he faced with the wind, he also felt strangely weak.

"I could tell from my practice kicks that my leg just wasn't as strong as usual," he said later. "And the wind was really playing tricks with the ball. I thought for sure I was going to have one of those days where nothing goes right."

The Cardinals, who had won the coin toss, chose to receive. Taking the ball on their own 23-yard line, they marched straight up the field until they were stopped on the Steeler 11. On fourth down and 8 yards to go, Bakken came in and lined up, as usual, 10 yards behind center Bob DeMarco and 3 behind holder Larry Wilson. He was going to try an 18-yard field goal. Ignoring the screams of more than 45,000 Steeler fans (who were telling their team to "Block that kick!"), he strode toward the ball as it was snapped. The Steeler defense strained mightily to get to the kicker before he could get the ball away. The Cardinal blockers strained just as mightily to keep the Steelers out. Out there in the middle of the field the noise of the crowd was

Square-toed Bakken waits to be called upon for a field goal or an extra point.

just a distant roar as the huge linemen came together—bodies, arms and legs flying every which way. Leather pads smacked together with a pop that could be heard on the sidelines, and animal-like grunts came from lips clenched behind face masks.

Bakken, however, heard and saw none of the

warfare surrounding him. A kicker cannot be distracted by anything if he is to do his job correctly. The St. Louis kicker knew what he had to do. He kept his head down, his eyes focused strictly on that part of the ball with which he had to make contact. As he booted it, he resisted the temptation to look up, a temptation that lures every kicker, and instead concentrated on his follow-through.

He had done his job properly. The football split the goal posts perfectly and sailed far beyond the end zone. The referee shot his arms straight up in the air, the scoreboard flashed three points for St. Louis and the crowd quieted to a murmur. Bakken trotted up field to kick off, the clock showed that only 5:44 had passed.

His kickoff, high but not too deep, came down on Pittsburgh's 15-yard line and was returned to the 27. The Steelers got to their 40, but on a third-and-9 play, quarterback Bill Nelsen was snowed under by Cardinals as he tried to pass. The ball popped loose, and St. Louis tackle Chuck Walker gleefully fell on it at the Steeler 34. The Cardinals ran six plays to get to the 17, where they were stopped. Bakken came in and booted his second field goal to boost the St. Louis lead to 6-0. Only 10:11 had elapsed in the game. Bakken no longer felt weak, and the wind didn't worry him any more. "When you get two that fast, you begin to feel like Superman," he said later. "I felt like thanking the Steelers for giving me the opportunity."

Out came the tee. Bakken moved into the ball and away it sailed, high and far this time down to the Steeler 1-yard line, where it was caught and returned to the 22. This time the Steelers were able to run only two plays before giving the ball away. Pat Fischer, the talented Cardinal safetyman, intercepted a Nelsen pass on the Steeler 43. St. Louis took maximum advantage of the break by taking the ball all the way in for a touchdown. Bakken, whose Number 25 jersey was by now quite familiar to the Steeler fans, came in and kicked the extra point. Happily for the Steelers, the first quarter ended a few seconds later. Perhaps they could pull themselves together and elimate their mistakes in the second period.

They could not. Fischer stole the ball right out of the hands of Steeler fullback Bill Asbury on the very first play, giving the Cardinals the ball on Pittsburgh's 47. But they could only manage to move 4 yards in three plays. So Bakken came in to try a 50-yard field goal, which, if made, would be only 1 yard shorter than the longest he had ever kicked. (The longest ever kicked in the NFL was 56 yards, by Bert Rechichar of the Baltimore Colts in 1953.)

Up went the ball, arching in a huge semicircle that ended with its descent near the goal line. The crowd was breathless as they watched it drop, for obviously it would be close. The ball fell 3 yards short, bringing a sigh of relief from both the Pitts-

Jim, with Larry Wilson (8) holding, shows the proper way to kick field goals during the game against the Steelers.

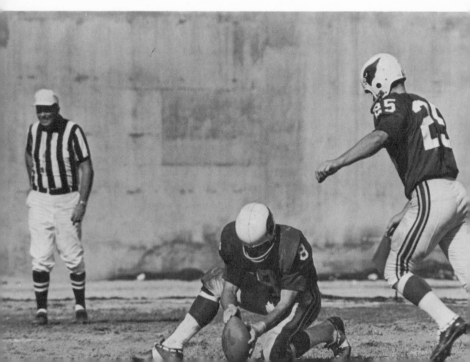

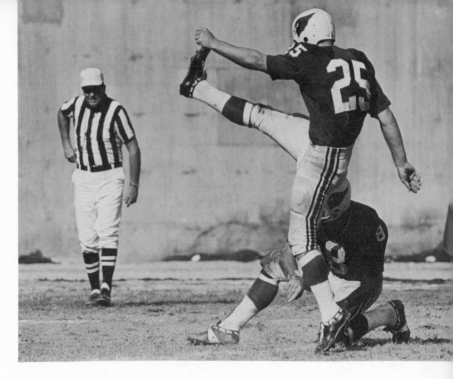

burgh players and fans. Perhaps this would mark the turning point. It didn't. Less than three minutes after his near miss, Bakken split the goal posts from 33 yards out to give St. Louis a 16-0 lead. Another Fischer interception had set it up.

"I'll keep catching them and you keep kicking them," Fischer said to Bakken on the sidelines. Overhearing his teammates, Wilson asked, "Don't I get any credit for holding the ball?" Obviously, the Cardinals were in good spirits.

Those spirits were dampened somewhat by a Steeler touchdown near the end of the period, but it was only a temporary setback. Immediately after the Pittsburgh score, the Cardinals began a march of their own, driving to the Steelers' 22 as the first half neared its end. With just twenty-six seconds to go, Bakken drove the ball through the uprights from 29 yards out for field goal Number 4 and the Cardinals had a 19-7 lead.

In the locker room later, Bakken thought about Yepremian's record and weighed the possibility of his matching or bettering it. With four field goals already on the scoreboard, he knew he had a chance.

But his cautious optimism had practically disappeared as the third quarter came to a close. The aroused Steelers, eager to atone for their first-half mistakes, dominated the play. They scored a touchdown to cut the Cardinal lead to five points, 19-14, and stopped Bakken completely. Not that shutting out the red-hot St. Louis kicker was easy, even for a determined Pittsburgh team. Bakken's only field-goal attempt of the quarter, a 45-yarder, missed by inches. In fact, Steeler defensive back Brady Keys had to jump at the goal line and bat the ball down. "I was sure I had it," Bakken said. "I think the wind shifted at the last second and held the ball up just enough to make it short."

In the fourth quarter, Bakken got off to a good start. With just forty-one seconds gone, he booted a 24-yard field goal, his fifth of the day and only one short of tying the NFL record. Perhaps he would achieve his miracle after all. As in the first half, he had the Steelers to thank for his success, for they suddenly reverted to their earlier errant ways. A poor 24-yard punt by Pittsburgh late in the third quarter had given the Cardinals the ball on the

Steeler 49-yard line. St. Louis quickly marched to the 17, where the drive stalled in the opening minute of the final period. This had given Bakken his opportunity for Number 5.

"You never kicked better in your life," said one dirty, grass-stained Pittsburgh lineman as he trotted past Bakken. The Cardinal kicker had to smile at his Steeler foe, for he knew the man was right.

Pittsburgh, now behind 22-14, was forced to play catch-up football, which meant the Steelers had to take chances. The Steelers took the kickoff and moved to their 42 in four plays. There, Nelsen rushed a pass and again had it intercepted, this time by Cardinal cornerback Bobby Williams. Williams ran the ball all the way back to the Steeler 38. Bakken watched with growing excitement as his teammates moved the ball down to the 26 before being stopped. On fourth-and-11, with 6:27 gone, Bakken entered the game to try for the field goal that would match Yepremian's record. "I was real confident," he said. "There was no indecision, no hesitation." The ball soared straight through the goal posts from 32 yards out. Bakken had matched the NFL record.

But before he even had the chance to let it sink in, much less celebrate, he was trotting back onto the field to try for a record-breaking seventh field goal. Again, a Pittsburgh lapse gave him his chance. After Bakken's sixth three-pointer, the Steelers took the kickoff, ran three plays and were forced to punt. Roy Shivers received the kick for the Cardinals, eluded the Steeler defense, and returned the ball all the way to Pittsburgh's 23-yard line. Three plays netted the Cardinals only 6 yards. On fourth down, Bakken found himself in excellent position: he would kick from the 23-yard line.

There was a little more than five minutes to play when he trotted onto the field. The teams lined up, the ball was snapped, and once again the two lines collided with savage force. "Concentrate," Bakken told himself as he approached the ball. "Don't pick up your head. Follow through." Sound advice— except that he ignored it. His foot had just made contact when he jerked his head up to follow the flight of the ball. "I was too excited," he said. "I wanted so badly to see if it was good that I violated one of the basic rules of kicking."

But Jim Bakken didn't suffer from his mistake. The ball arched high in the gray haze hanging over Pitt Stadium and flew straight through the goal posts. The record was his.

14/The Day the Jets Were Super

MIAMI: January 12, 1969—"We'll win. I'll guarantee it."

The words of New York Jets quarterback Joe Namath, spoken boldly and brashly at a banquet earlier in the week, were now on the line as the Jets and the Baltimore Colts trotted through pregame drills before the Super Bowl showdown.

Many people thought this third Super Bowl championship football game could be the most interesting one simply because of Namath's presence. But the American Football League Jets were still heavy 18-point underdogs to the Colts, who had ravaged the rest of the National Football League during the previous four months.

Such odds, however, did not bother Namath, and as 75,377 fans climbed to their seats in the Orange Bowl and as 65 million fans lined up in front of their television sets, many pondered the remarks the Jet quarterback had made during the past week.

"There are at least four quarterbacks in our league who are better than Earl Morrall," Namath had said, referring to Baltimore's starting signal caller, the man who had replaced the great Johnny Unitas and his sore elbow for the entire season. "There's Daryle Lamonica, John Hadl, Bob Griese and myself. In fact, you put Babe Parilli with Baltimore, and Baltimore might be better. Babe throws better than Morrall."

Namath's statement about Morrall had been insulting enough to the Colts, because Morrall had finished the season as the NFL's leading passer and its Most Valuable Player. But to compare Parilli, the Jets' aging reserve quarterback, to Morrall was downright outrageous.

Lou Michaels was one of the Colts who had been particularly outraged. In fact, Namath had aroused his ire in person. The Colt place-kicker and substitute defensive end had run into the Jet superstar the previous Sunday at a restaurant in Fort Lauderdale, where both teams were staying. Both coaches, New York's Weeb Ewbank and Baltimore's Don Shula, had given their players the day off and suspended the curfew before the teams began their serious workouts for the game.

When Michaels and some teammates arrived at the restaurant, a short distance from the beach and the Atlantic Ocean, Namath and Jet safety Jim Hudson already were there.

"We're going to kick the heck out of you guys,"

Joe Namath (12) lets a pass go against the stunned Colts.

Namath told Michaels after they had said hello.

"Haven't you ever heard of the word modesty, Joseph?" Michaels asked.

"We're going to beat you and pick you apart," Namath shot back.

"If you fellows do, Joseph, I believe you are the man to do it," the Colt said. "It's kind of hard, though, throwing out of a well and finding receivers."

"Don't worry about that," Joe replied. "My blockers will give me time."

Eventually Michaels was so infuriated he invited Namath out to the parking lot. "I'll knock your head off," the 250-pound Michaels told the 195-pound Namath. However, Dan Sullivan, a Colt guard, stepped in and cooled things down. They all sat down together and, when it was time to leave, Namath stunned Michaels by pulling out a $100 bill to pay for everything.

The next day, however, Namath had to pay out an additional fifty dollars because he slept late and missed a picture-taking session. Teammates Matt Snell and Emerson Boozer also missed it and were fined $50 each by Coach Weeb Ewbank.

That same day, the story of the confrontation between Michaels and Namath quickly spread through the two camps—the Jets at Yankee Stadium in Fort Lauderdale and the Colts at St. Andrews School in Boca Raton.

"He talks too much," said Billy Ray Smith, the

Colt defensive tackle, an eleven-year veteran. "When it comes to throwing the football, I have to put him up there with the best I've ever seen. But he should keep his mouth shut. He'll keep his teeth a lot longer."

Controversy was nothing new to Joe Namath, the black-haired son of a Hungarian immigrant. Ever since 1965 when Sonny Werblin, the Jet president, signed him out of the University of Alabama to a contract worth $427,000, Namath had been the center of attention. And certainly the Jet star had done nothing to discourage the attention. On the field, he wore white shoes. Off the field, he had been seen wearing a $5,000 mink coat which he received for doing a commercial. In 1968, he also added a Fu Manchu mustache which lasted for weeks until he was paid $10,000 to shave it off for another television commercial. The white llama rug and oval bed in his plush East Side apartment in New York City were legendary.

But none of these off-field activities and decorations detracted from his play on the field. In fact, he had led the Jets to the Super Bowl, firing them to eleven victories in fourteen games, plus a 27-23 victory over the Oakland Raiders in the AFL championship game.

During that title game, when the Raiders went ahead, 23-20, Namath walked over to Coach Ewbank on the sidelines and said, "Don't worry, we'll get it back." They did, of course.

But even though he had proved that his confidence and determination were not bluff, knowledgeable football people still thought him brash when he assessed the Baltimore Colts and proclaimed: "We'll win. I'll guarantee it."

During the regular season the Colts had shut out three opponents and allowed ten or less points in seven other games. Then they defeated Minnesota, 24-14 for the NFL Western Conference title and annihilated Cleveland, 34-0 for the NFL crown.

In the two previous Super Bowls, the NFL Green Bay Packers had soundly crushed Kansas City and Oakland, turning the first two world championship contests into great NFL victories. Now, with clouds dotting the sky and the temperature in the seventies, the Colts kicked off with plans to continue the NFL's success.

Matt Snell started New York moving by hitting the Colt left tackle twice for 12 yards and a first down. Two plays later, Namath passed to Snell for 9 yards, but on third down the fullback lost 2 yards, and Curley Johnson had to punt.

Although the Colt offense was not considered as potent as the defense, possibly the best player on the team was John Mackey, the brilliant tight end. On Baltimore's first play, Morrall threw the ball to Mackey, and the 6-foot 2-inch, 224-pound veteran powered his way for 19 yards before tackle John Elliott caught up with him and pulled him down. The Colts continued to make it look easy, racing for three more first downs and reaching the New York 19. They certainly played as if the oddsmakers had known what they were talking about.

Suddenly, however, the Colts bogged down. Morrall missed on two passes, then gained nothing on a third-down run up the middle.

Lou Michaels, whose brother, Walt, was the Jet defensive backfield coach, came in for a field-goal try from the 27, but he missed and the Jets had a reprieve. Neither team could do anything the next time it had the ball, but the Colts put New York in a hole when David Lee punted dead at the Jet 4. With third-and-1, Namath made a good move to get out of the hole, hitting George Sauer at the 16. But the split end fumbled the ball when cornerback Lenny Lyles hit him, and Colt linebacker Ron Porter recovered at the New York 12.

Jeery Hill lost a yard on the last play of the first quarter, but Tom Matte circled left end for 7, and Morrall dropped back to pass. He fired to tight end Tom Mitchell at the left of the goal posts in the end zone, but the ball hit the receiver on the right shoulder pad, bounded high in the air and came down into the arms of Randy Beverly, a second-year cornerback. Again, a reprieve for the Jets.

Getting the ball at the 20, Namath, who hadn't done anything in the first quarter to fulfill his guarantee, decided to test the right side of the Colts' defense. Snell, who had come back successfully from knee surgery the previous season, took the ball

Matt Snell (41) drives through the Colt line for

one of his many gains, as Bill Mathis (31) leads way.

four straight times. And four straight times he went through or around the Colts' right side. He gained 1, 7, 6 and 12 yards, and the Jets had two first downs, the second at their 46.

While the Colts' right side was still trying to catch its breath, Namath threw one incomplete pass but then struck for 6 yards to Billy Mathis, 14 to Sauer and 11 to Sauer, moving the ball to the Baltimore 23. Halfback Emerson Boozer ran for 2, and Namath hit Snell for 12 and a first down at the 9.

On first down Namath crossed up the Colts by sending Snell to their left side for a 5-yard gain as guard Randy Rasmussen and tackle Dave Herman effectively held off the Smiths—end Bubba and tackle Billy Ray. Snell took the ball again on the next play but this time through the right side behind Boozer, who cut down linebacker Don Shinnick and sprang the fullback into the end zone. Jim Turner kicked the extra point, and for the first time the AFL representative led the NFL team in a Super Bowl, 7-0. The Colts were less stunned than annoyed that this team they were supposed to handle with ease had scored first.

On the other hand, it was most satisfying to Jet Coach Weeb Ewbank, who had coached the Colts for nine years before being replaced by Don Shula. Weeb had led the Colts to their last previous championships in 1958 and 1959. In fact, nine of the twenty-two Colt starters this day had once played for Ewbank, and the roly-poly man who resembled a grandfather more than a football coach had drafted five others. He had even coached Shula when the Baltimore coach played for Cleveland and Baltimore in the 1950's.

Now Ewbank watched his fired-up Jets stymie another Colt drive as Michaels missed another field-goal try, this one from the 46. Turner, however, also missed one, from the 41, and the Colts had the ball again.

On second down, halfback Matte scampered around right end, ran over two Jets and raced 58

Defensive back Johnny Sample (42) brashly holds up the ball after making an interception.

yards to the New York 16. But after Hill gained a yard, Johnny Sample made a diving, tumbling interception of Morrall's pass to flanker Willie Richardson at the 2-yard line. This was the same Sample who played on Baltimore's title teams in 1958-59 but who now was considered by many to be the weak link in the Jet secondary.

By now, Morrall, who finally had found success with the Colts after twelve years of part-time quarterbacking with four other teams, felt harassed. The next time he got the ball he tried a little razzle-dazzle to shake up the Jets and get them off his back. On second down at the New York 41, he handed to Matte, who started running to his right. The halfback stopped, however, and threw the ball back to Morrall. By this time, split end Jimmy Orr, had eluded cornerback Beverly and was standing all alone on the left side near the goal line. But Morrall was looking toward the right side and threw to Hill instead. This time safety Jim Hudson picked off the pass, and the half ended with five pass completions and three interceptions for Morrall.

The second half started just as badly for Baltimore. On the first play Matte fumbled, and Jet linebacker Ralph Baker fell on the ball at the Baltimore 33. The Jets proceeded to eat up nearly five minutes of playing time before Turner kicked a 32-yard field goal for a 10-0 lead. Three passes by Morrall were futile and soon Turner was back on the field to boot

Johnny Unitas, an old hero in Baltimore, is called upon to rally the trampled Colts.

a 30-yard field goal, raising the score to 13-0.

The Colts continued to try to break through the Jet defense, but they were able to hold the ball for only eight plays in the entire third quarter. Even Johnny Unitas, whom Shula in desperation sent in for Morrall, couldn't spur the Colts on.

Four plays into the fourth quarter Turner, who owns thirteen pairs of football shoes, kicked a 9-yard field goal. The Jets were ahead, 16-0.

Unitas came back on the field with the Colt offensive unit. A sore elbow had limited Unitas to 32 pass attempts all season but he had led the Colts to so many great moments in the past that Shula felt the gamble was worth it. Unitas used the running of Matte and Hill to move the ball to the New York 25. There, on second down, Unitas' pass was intercepted by Beverly in the end zone for the Jets' fourth steal of the day.

But after Turner missed a 42-yard field goal try with six minutes left in the game, Unitas finally ignited the Colts. He missed his first three passes, then connected with Orr for 17 yards. He threw two more errant tosses, then completed an 11-yarder to Mackey. Two more passes, for 21 yards to Richardson and 11 to Orr, put Baltimore at the Jets' 2. New York's defense stopped Unitas and Matte on the first two downs, but Hill finally bucked across from the 1.

After fifty-six minutes and forty-one seconds, the Colts finally had scored, and now they had just 199

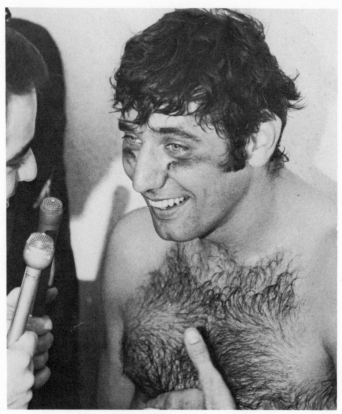

A happy winner, Joe Namath, talks it up.

seconds to beat the Jets, something they were supposed to have done as early as the first quarter.

The Jets, of course, expected a short kickoff, and
Lou Michaels did just that. But Baltimore's Mitchell fell on the ball at the New York 44, and suddenly
Colt hopes burst alive. Shula stayed with Unitas
even though the brilliant thirteen-year veteran
couldn't throw long because of the elbow he had

hurt in the final exhibition game in September.

Unitas passed to Richardson for 6, to Orr for 14, to Richardson for 5. Colt fans stirred. Was it possible? Could football's premier quarterback actually pull it off and keep National League supremacy intact?

Unitas passed to Richardson. Sample broke it up. Unitas passed to Orr. It fell short. Unitas passed to Orr. It went too far. Suddenly it was the Jets' ball. The miracle of a Colt comeback had evaporated. Joe Namath didn't appear so foolish anymore.

The Jets had won, 16-7. Namath and his teammates had made good his guarantee.

INDEX